HIDDEN HISTORY *of* MONTGOMERY COUNTY, INDIANA

Jodie Steelman Wilson,
Emily Griffin Winfrey &
Rebecca McDole

The History Press

Published by The History Press
Charleston, SC 29403
www.historypress.net

Cover images courtesy of the Crawfordsville District Public Library.

First published 2012

Manufactured in the United States

ISBN 978.1.60949.522.0

Library of Congress Cataloging-in-Publication Data

Wilson, Jodie Steelman.
Hidden history of Montgomery County, Indiana / Jodie Steelman Wilson, Emily Griffin, and Rebecca McDole.
p. cm.
Includes bibliographical references and index.
ISBN 978-1-60949-522-0
1. Montgomery County (Ind.)--History--Anecdotes. 2. Montgomery County (Ind.)--History, Local--Anecdotes. 3. Montgomery County (Ind.)--Biography--Anecdotes. I. Griffin, Emily, 1984- II. McDole, Rebecca. III. Title.
F532.M75W55 2012
977.2'48--dc23
2012004818

Contents

Contents

Acknowledgements

The authors would like to thank the head of the Reference and Local History Department at the Crawfordsville District Public Library (CDPL), Bill Helling, for his support and extensive help throughout the entire process. We couldn't, and wouldn't, have done it without you! Dellie Craig was always willing to help us with any request, and her amazing memory for our collection items frequently came in handy. Thank you to our library director, Larry Hathaway, and our library board for their support in the production of this book; thanks also go to the many previous librarians and donors who created the rich local history collection we have at CDPL. Thank you to Joe Gartrell and The History Press for seeing the significance of our county's history and our contributions to the historical record; and thanks also to Ryan Finn, who guided us through completion. To all those who have helped us throughout this process, we are sincerely grateful.

A very special thank-you goes to the family members of our chapter subjects: Jeanne Ann Vanderhoef, for Maude Snyder; Stephen Goldman and Kathy Shimberg, for the Harry Freedman family; Sally Herr, Eleanor Herr, Ann White and Jeff Bennett, for Shirl Herr (and Nellie Coutant); the family of Lillian Lookabill Hodgson; Patrick Camblin, Roy Camblin and Nolia Brandt, for Mary Oda and Frederick Eglin; the members of the Boynton-Harbert Society, for Elizabeth Boynton Harbert; and Marjorie Ross and John Ross, for Malcolm Ross.

Thank you to our other sources: John Kummings and Mary Kummings for the Taft photograph; Barb Coghlin for details on Mary Oda Eglin and

Horace Hickam; Clay McCutchan, Eglin AFB historian; Maria Freire, for her permission to use the photograph of President Kennedy and Malcolm Ross taken by her late husband, Del Ankers; Eric Frye of the Crawfordsville Fire Department; Steve Loy and Donna Jeffers; Hubert Danzebrink and Sandy Lofland-Brown for courthouse details; and Mary Kay Duggan and Kathleen Correia for assistance with Hartman sheet music. Special thanks go to Karen Bazzani Zach for her recollection of Ruth Morgan and her knowledgeable responses to many questions on various local subjects throughout this project.

We also wish to thank Alison Wright of the Montgomery County Historical Society and Beth Swift, archivist at Lilly Library, Wabash College, for providing us access to information and photographs within their institutions' collections.

Emily would like to thank her husband and best friend, Russell, for his loving support and endless encouragement. Also deserving of mention are Emily's parents, sister and grandparents, who, although far apart in miles, have always been so closely devoted to her endeavors.

Jodie would like to thank her family—Michael, Annie and Ali—for their support during the writing of this book. Thank you to her parents, Keith and Sheila Steelman, for her years at the University of Illinois, where she learned to write for the public good, and to Professor Lou Liebovich, who taught her how.

Rebecca would like to thank all her family, especially her parents, Don and Deb, for their support and unfailing confidence in her. Thank you also to her best friends—Holly, Krissy and Tricia—for their encouragement and help with this project.

Introduction

Montgomery County, Indiana, never fails to surprise the visitor with its unique and varied history, but even local residents are often unaware of some of their county's heritage. Of course, anyone who spends some time in Crawfordsville will eventually know about General Lew Wallace, author of the longtime bestseller *Ben-Hur*, and Senator Henry Lane, who helped found the Republican Party and get Abraham Lincoln nominated for the presidency. However, *Hidden History of Montgomery County, Indiana* strives to bring to light many of the area's other deserving stories. Much research on Montgomery County has been done, but it does not always provide information on lesser-known people, places and events. Nevertheless, this book should not be viewed as a comprehensive hidden history—there are many more fascinating stories to tell and people to explore. You may also wonder why a local figure or event you expected to find is not listed here. Many worthy people and occurrences are not reported in this book simply because they have often been documented and are readily available elsewhere. In addition, we have only so much room and can't include everything we would like. Realize, too, that the facts we present may not match existing publications either online or in print; we have made great efforts to use primary sources, we have found additional family information and we have enhanced previous histories.

Our current research would not be possible without patrons' donations of historical documents, photographs and family histories to the Crawfordsville District Public Library's local history collection and archives. Fortunately, the majority of our primary documents had been retained and protected at the library, which is committed to preserving the rich history of Montgomery County for future generations. Through the library's online local history databases (www.cdpl.lib.in.us/lh), CDPL is able to share its vast collection of resources with descendants and researchers around the world.

We must admit that none of us is a native of Montgomery County, but working in a county with such an impressive and colorful background has led us to embrace this county as our own. As reference and local history librarians, we are fortunate to hear firsthand accounts from residents and uncover never-before-published gems in our archives on a daily basis. We are continuously discovering new stories about our adopted county, whether in documents that have been hidden for one hundred years or in oral histories that are simply new to our nonlocal ears. Our enthusiasm for local research has grown as we see the twinkle in the eye and hear the excitement in the voice of a resident remembering a president's speech on a train, a movie star's stop at the local milkshake bar or his or her grandfather's downtown business. Without the willingness of these individuals, recording the history of Montgomery County would prove futile. If not for the generous people who share their stories, photos and documents with us every day, these historic artifacts and precious memories would be lost forever. Furthermore, we are fortunate to work in a community where historical organizations and societies collaborate, support one another and share one common goal: the preservation of our county's heritage.

We hope you understand that in our Reference and Local History Department, we have many tasks besides historical and genealogical research to occupy our time. These other various tasks and responsibilities are too numerous to list here. However, the satisfaction we receive from our local history work is immeasurable, and helping patrons with their needs is one of our most enjoyable activities. Although the library began to add local history information to the collection long ago, clippings and other early items often are missing the name of the source and date published. For this reason, some sources mentioned in the chapters of this book lack full citation information, but we are grateful that these items were retained for the future. Also, local newspaper titles varied over the years, so we have chosen a consistent style throughout this book. It is our hope that we may continue to build on the early foundation laid by librarians long ago and that future researchers will benefit from the research we continue to add. Our final wish is that those who follow us inherit the same interest and desire to serve the residents of Montgomery County.

The Highest Achiever of Linden High School

Jodie Steelman Wilson

If it hadn't been for astronaut Alan Shepard, Linden High School graduate Malcolm Ross might have received widespread public recognition for his greatest achievement, the Strato-Lab 5 balloon flight. At 9:47 a.m. on May 4, 1961, Ross and co-pilot Dr. (and lieutenant commander) Victor Prather set a new world record for the highest manned balloon flight in history, achieving an altitude of 21.5 miles. Their mission was a necessary step on the way to manned space flight because its primary purpose was the high-altitude testing of space suits to be used by Project Mercury astronauts. Not even twenty-four hours later, before daily newspapers had a chance to proclaim their accomplishment, Alan Shepard became the first American in space. Coverage of Ross and Prather's achievement was buried by the news of the successful space flight that they had helped to ensure.

But Ross was a commander in the Naval Reserve and a former active officer in the U.S. Navy. He wasn't motivated by public recognition. He had a duty to perform, and he completed this mission just as he had the eight others he had been assigned. However, this flight would present more challenges than any previous flight and would prove to be the last for both Ross and Prather.

In a *National Geographic* account of the Strato-Lab 5 flight published in the November 1961 issue, Ross wrote of his awareness of the risks of the high-altitude flight, including extreme cold and extreme low pressure. A failure

The official U.S. Navy photograph of Commander Malcolm D. Ross, dated 1959. Ross graduated from Linden High School in 1936 and married Linden High School classmate Marjorie Martin in 1941. *Collection of Mrs. Marjorie Ross.*

of the space suit or protective faceplate would have meant a quick death to the wearer. According to Shirley Thomas in her book *Men of Space*, for these reasons Ross considered the mission the "most hazardous flight ever made." Still, Ross was confident: "When I tell you I know a system well, I know it

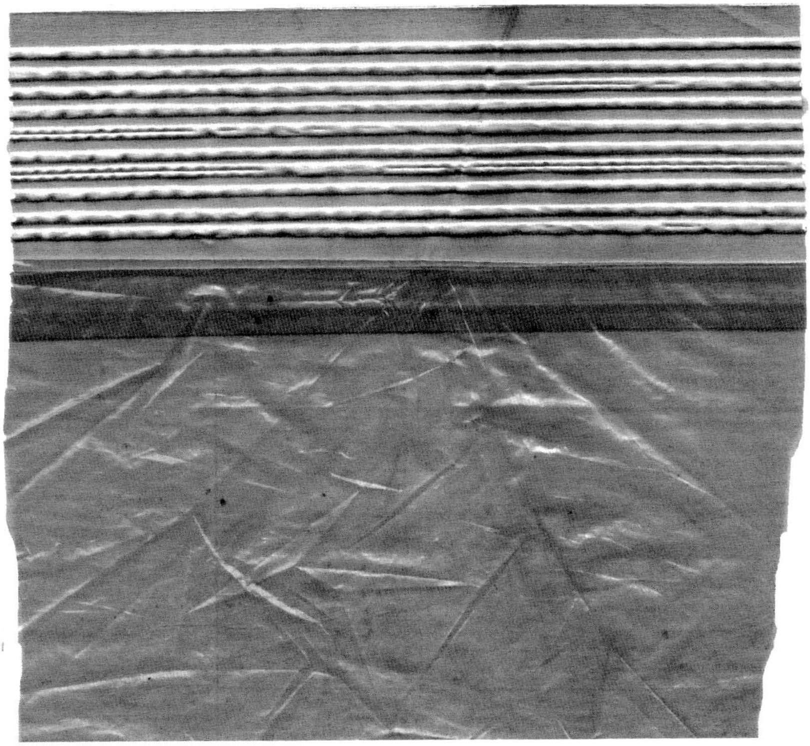

A piece of the balloon that carried Malcolm D. Ross and Victor Prather to the record books during their Strato-Lab 5 flight. The thin polyethylene material resembles a kitchen plastic storage bag, and any necessary repairs were made to the balloon with common transparent adhesive tape. *Collection of Mrs. Marjorie Ross.*

very well. I know every component, every piece, I know what the chances of success and failure are of individual components. I realize the balloon itself is the weakest link."

The balloon was constructed of polyethylene material only one-thousandth of an inch in thickness, and Ross knew well the limitations of these balloons at high altitudes. After ascending to fifty-four thousand feet, the temperature would drop to ninety-four degrees (Fahrenheit) below zero. Ross wrote in his *Geographic* account, "We knew that our balloon now was as brittle as a glass Christmas tree ornament…a wind shear—could shatter it into confetti."

Lightning was also a grave concern. In the same article, Ross noted that a year earlier, an unmanned balloon had been struck by lightning, causing the gondola to be dropped. However, motivated by the need to determine the exact capability of the space suits, Ross and Prather willingly embarked on the most rigorous testing of space suits ever performed outside a laboratory: a dangerous nine-hour flight into the stratosphere.

The balloon was launched at 7:08 a.m. on the morning of May 4, 1961, from the deck of the USS *Antietam* in the Gulf of Mexico. Just after 7:30 a.m., the balloon reached 26,000 feet, a critical moment in the flight. To survive above this altitude, the pilots wore suits that needed to pressurize quickly. They waited; nothing happened. The balloon cleared 26,500 feet. Still the suits did not respond. After 27,000 feet, they finally began to hear the pressure valves releasing, and the suits held pressure as designed—a huge relief for the pilots. But minutes later, Ross heard a hissing sound that he feared was a leak in his space suit. At the same time, the balloon began to slow in its climb, creating concern that the balloon itself was leaking. Then the radio connection to the *Antietam* went dead.

Broadcasting to any nearby ship, the pair tried to reach help, but to no avail. Finally, the balloon entered warmer air, and things improved quickly. The balloon resumed its rapid climb, communications with the ship returned and even the inexplicable hiss stopped. And it was just in time. Shortly after the balloon cleared seventy-one thousand feet, the newly resumed communication link saved Victor Prather's life when he was warned by the monitoring team on the ship that his protective faceplate was overheating. A twin indicator light on the balloon itself had failed to light, and the pilots were unaware of the threat. Had this warning been missed, the suit would have lost pressure, killing Prather.

At 100,000 feet, the pilots were able to enjoy a view few other humans have ever seen: four hundred miles of the United States of America displayed to the horizon. At a higher altitude, the state of Florida lay in full view before them. Then an update came from the *Antietam*: Ross and Prather had broken the previous record for a highest altitude balloon flight at their current altitude. Ross recalled in his *National Geographic* article that with the view they were enjoying, "I had forgotten all about the record. Somehow it seems rather insignificant."

Although the record had been set, Ross and Prather were not yet out of danger. The descent was a difficult balance: lose too much helium and the balloon would drop like a stone, but lose too little and their oxygen would deplete before their flight had descended to a safe altitude. But after the balloon had descended too slowly for half an hour, Ross was forced to be more aggressive. By the time the descent became fast enough, the balloon entered warmer air, which accelerated the balloon's drop to more than 1,140 feet per minute. Ballast, heavy supplies and even a dragline necessary for a landing on the aircraft carrier were jettisoned overboard. By 7,000 feet, the pilots had slowed the descent to a comfortable pace, and they relaxed with cigarettes as they waited for their landing.

After the gondola's splashdown in the Gulf of Mexico, with the monitoring crew on the USS *Antietam* only a mile and a half away, the flight appeared a complete success. The navy was now confident that the space suits would protect high-altitude pilots, and Ross and Prather had set a world record that still stands at the time of this writing. It had been a productive mission in many ways. But as the helicopters arrived to return the pilots to the *Antietam*, an unforeseen tragedy occurred. Ross was evacuated first, at the insistence of Prather. But when Prather's own turn came, his hands slipped from the rescue hook, and he fell into the water and drowned before navy rescue divers could reach him.

Ross wrote of the outcome of their flight in *National Geographic*, "Our flight means that mankind can advance with more confidence toward undreamed-of wonders in the universe. The priceless knowledge we gained is Vic's memorial. He earned it with courage and devotion in the perilous emptiness where space begins." While Ross saw to it that Victor Prather's name was known for the advances he helped to make, in Montgomery County, Ross's own local connection went unrecognized. The May 5, 1961 *Crawfordsville Journal Review* featured a two-line headline, all capitals, regarding the Alan Shepard flight that ran from one page edge to the other: "'BOY, WHAT A RIDE!' U.S. ASTRONAUT SAYS AFTER ROCKET RIDE INTO SPACE." A small one-column article beneath it read, "Accident Kills U.S. Balloonist After Record." The Associated Press article summarizing the flight mentioned only that Ross was a former resident of West Lafayette.

Even after Malcolm Ross spoke at the Linden High School alumni banquet just a few weeks after his record-breaking flight, the *Journal Review* of May 22, 1961, carried the news as an AP story, picked up from a wire service rather than written by a staff reporter. The brief coverage included a photograph of Ross at the banquet, which ran on page eight of the section. About a week later, the *Lafayette Journal and Courier* ran its coverage of Ross's speech at the Linden alumni banquet with a full-page story complete with many quotes, a photograph and a detailed look at his recent record-breaking flight.

While the rest of the county might not have known Ross, Linden did. Although he was born in Momence, Illinois, he spent his childhood in West Lafayette. About 1932, Ross's parents bought a farm near Linden, and he attended all four years of high school there, graduating in 1936. He played baseball and basketball, sang in the church choir and participated in many

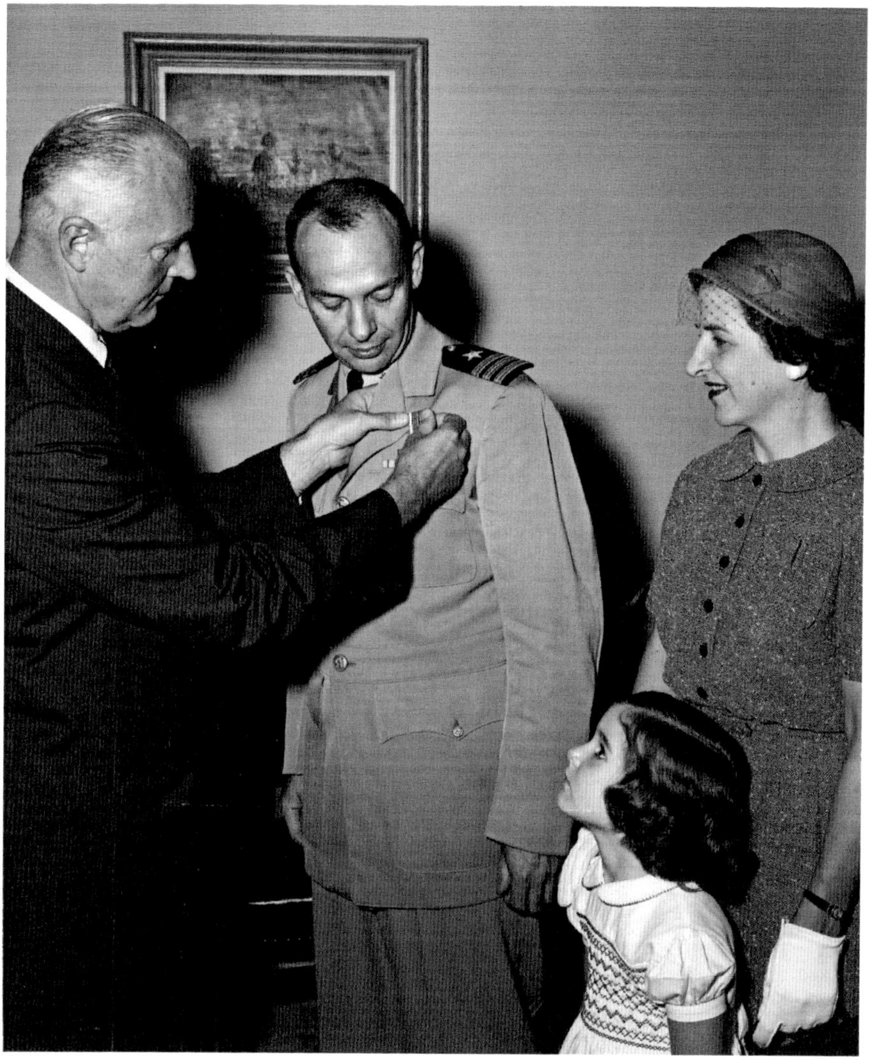

Commander Malcolm D. Ross receives his first Distinguished Flying Cross (he was awarded two) from James H. Wakelin, assistant secretary of the navy for research and development. His wife, Marjorie, and daughter, Jane, look on. Official U.S. Navy photo. *Collection of Mrs. Marjorie Ross.*

high school activities with classmate Marjorie Martin, whom he married in 1941 after his graduation from Purdue University.

But even if most of Montgomery County had missed the significance of Malcolm Ross's career, it was recognized by others. Ross's efforts were critical to the navy's development of experimental manned balloon missions, Project Strato-Lab. He and Lieutenant Commander Lee Lewis received the

John Fitzgerald Kennedy awards the Harmon International Trophies in the White House Rose Garden on October 18, 1962. Commander Malcolm D. Ross and Victor Prather (posthumously) were awarded the 1962 Harmon International Trophy for aeronauts for their world-record Strato-Lab 5 flight. In a row behind the president, *from left*, are Lieutenant Colonel William R. Payne, Ross, aviatrix Jacqueline Cochran, Mrs. Virginia Prather (widow of Victor Prather) and Marjorie Ross. The children of Ross and Prather stand to the front left of the photo. *Photo by Del Ankers.*

Harmon International Trophy for their 1956 balloon flight for setting a new altitude record for a manned balloon, and Ross was awarded both the Rear Admiral William S. Parsons Award for Scientific and Technical Progress and the United States Navy Meritorious Civilian Service Award in 1957. In 1958, he was awarded his first Distinguished Flying Cross. He received a Special Award given by the American Meteorological Society in 1960.

In 1962, he received his second Harmon International Trophy, awarded jointly with Victor Prather. In a ceremony at the White House, John F. Kennedy presented the trophy, and Prather's wife, Virginia Merritt Prather, accepted it on behalf of her husband.

Ross received a Gold Star in lieu of a second Distinguished Flying Cross award for his 1961 flight, the citation reading in part, "For heroism and extraordinary achievement while participating in a balloon flight on 4 May

1961...Through his outstanding professional ability, courage, and devotion to duty, he made a significant contribution to...the United States in the fields of flight in upper air and in space. His conduct throughout was in keeping with the finest traditions of the United States Naval Service."

As he announced at the Linden High School alumni banquet in 1961, Ross left military service in 1961 but continued working in space research for General Motors, and later he directed his own space research company. He died on October 8, 1985, and is buried at Arlington National Cemetery near his friend and colleague Victor Prather.

Spooks, Specters and Spirit Photographs

Rebecca McDole

Ghost stories. They are staples around campfires and at slumber parties. Whether you believe them or not, practically everyone has heard one, and every town has its haunted houses, hospitals or cemeteries. In the nineteenth century, ghost stories took on a life of their own, growing into a social and religious movement and sparking a lively pastime in Montgomery County.

Spiritualism emerged at a time when people were trying to reconcile science and religion. The basic beliefs at the heart of spiritualism were that the soul survived after death and that communication with spirits was possible through mediums. The spiritualist movement began in Hydesville, New York, in 1848 when the Fox family began hearing unexplained sounds. Sisters Margaret, fifteen, and Kate, twelve, convinced their parents that the rapping sounds were made by spirits and that the girls could communicate with the spirits. Their story caught the public's interest, and the girls soon became famous mediums. Séances became popular as public performances and as private events; spiritualist journals were abundant, and mediums were discovered in every corner of life.

Robert Dale Owen, the son of New Harmony founder Robert Owen, began spreading spiritualism in Indiana in the 1850s. Churches began to spring up all over the state, the first being in Fountain County, near Veedersburg. The first state organization of spiritualists was formed in 1862. The Indiana Association of Spiritualists, formed in 1888, opened Camp

Chesterfield on the banks of the White River in 1891. Camp Chesterfield, a spiritualist church, is still in operation today. Meanwhile, in Montgomery County, spiritualism caught on in a big way in 1869.

The *Crawfordsville Weekly Journal* reported on October 23 that a "large number of spiritual circles have been organized in our city. New mediums are daily being developed." Invitations were extended to mediums and healers to come to Crawfordsville; Dr. Keith, "Spiritual Magnetic Healer," arrived in the city on October 27 to restore sight to the blind and make the deaf hear and the lame leap for joy, all at no charge. A distinguished lecturer, Mr. R. Graves spoke at the courthouse in November on "The Moral, Religious, and Spiritual Developments of the Nineteenth Century," and Madam Von Gobert, a "celebrated clairvoyant," stayed in November at the Richardson House hotel, where she shared her "wonderful and miraculous" knowledge of past and future events. The *Weekly Journal* said on November 11, 1869, "Our city has been overrun for the last week with Spiritual mediums."

But not all mediums wanted notoriety. The *Crawfordsville Weekly Review* mentioned on November 27, 1869, that a new medium was discovering his talents. Skeptical of spiritualism, this reluctant medium, who preferred to remain anonymous, was said to be possessed of wonderful and inexplicable powers, a demonstration of which would take place in a private séance. Séances continued to draw crowds after 1869. Miss Keyser held one or two in 1871 but was unsuccessful in communicating with spirits. A séance was held at the Opera House at 18 North Washington Street in 1882 by Professor Slade, but the *Crawfordsville Star* reported that the people were disappointed in him.

A more successful venture occurred on March 23, 1882, at the Opera House. Mr. Brown, a mind reader, played to a modest audience. The *Star* was of the opinion that the crowd would have been bigger if people could have been sure that it was *the* Brown, as they had been "gulled here so often by humbugs." Nevertheless, it was a "rather riotous spiritual séance." Brown invited a committee onstage to watch for tricks, and an unidentified "itinerant doctor and alleged magician of this city" caused a stir with his antics. He was "cat-called, whistled at, hooted and snored at, and not allowed to take a seat on the stage." He then claimed he could control his wife by mind reading, prompting an offended spiritualist to rush the stage.

When Brown was finally allowed to take the stage, he astounded his audience. Blindfolded, Brown placed his hand on a subject's forehead and asked him to think of a random man in the audience. The medium described the man perfectly and even stumbled through the audience to place his

Fisher Doherty, businessman, altruist, abolitionist and spiritualist, manufactured carriages and buggies. At the time this ad was printed in the *Crawfordsville Weekly Journal* in 1870, Doherty and his partner, Deighton, were located on Washington Street, opposite Center Church. *CDPL Photo.*

hand on the man's head as proof. Next, with his back turned, he asked a subject to write down the name of a dead relative with whom the subject wished to speak. Holding the folded-up paper, Brown described in detail the subject's deceased father, brother and nephew. The final act was a letdown, though. Brown attempted to read the mind of well-known local attorney John E. Humphreys, but the feat was an absolute failure.

The business of spirit photography began in 1861 with Boston jewelry engraver William H. Mumler, who found a ghostly image of a deceased cousin in a self-portrait. Spirit photographs are pictures supposed to show glimpses of the departed—ghostly images or unexplained lights appeared next to people in the photograph. Mary Todd Lincoln had her spirit photograph taken by Mumler; the image of the late Abraham Lincoln appeared behind her with his hands on her shoulders. Sir Arthur Conan Doyle was also an enthusiastic believer in spirit photography.

In Crawfordsville, spirit photography was a sensation thanks to two men, Fisher Doherty and A.D. Willis.

The *Crawfordsville Weekly Journal* called Fisher Doherty "the great apostle of spiritualism in this city" on August 10, 1871. When Doherty died, the *Weekly Journal* claimed on December 27, 1890, that "probably no citizen of the county was better known than Fisher Doherty." Born in Columbus, Ohio, in 1817, Doherty came in 1844 to Crawfordsville, where he and his sons built a prosperous business manufacturing wagons and carriages. Fisher was known for more than his business acumen; he was also an advocate of temperance reform in the city and was admired for his charitable works. The *Weekly Journal* noted that he would "long be remembered by the city's poor." He was probably most well known, though, for his work as an abolitionist. The *Weekly Journal* claimed in 1890 that Crawfordsville was a main station of the Underground Railroad and that Fisher Doherty's home was the stopping place for runaway slaves making their way north. "He is said to have assisted hundreds on their way and spent much time and money most cheerfully in this manner," reads Doherty's obituary in the *Weekly Journal* on December 27, 1890. He attended Center Presbyterian Church regularly, but he did not find that his belief in spiritualism undermined his faith.

When Fisher Doherty's path crossed with that of A.D. Willis, photographic magic happened. Abner Denman Willis, older brother of infamous Alamo doctor Joseph Martin "Doc" Willis, was born in Montgomery County in 1834. He operated a traveling photograph gallery before moving to Crawfordsville in 1866 and opening a gallery at 20 East Main Street. He earned a good reputation as an honest and conscientious photographer, but in 1869, Willis found that his artistic talents had taken an eerie turn. At first, when ghostly images appeared in pictures he had taken, he would "throw them on the floor in disgust," according to the *Weekly Journal* on December 9, 1869, and refuse to sit customers requesting a spirit photograph. But after some cajoling by Fisher Doherty and other prominent men, he accepted his role as photographic medium and opened his gallery to spiritualists.

John Booe, druggist of Moffett and Booe at 26 East Main Street, had his spirit photograph taken. The *Crawfordsville Weekly Review* reported on August 28, 1869, that what appeared to be the ghost of someone's grandmother hovered over his shoulder. Booe had his doubts—not about the presence of the ghost but rather that his guardian angel could look so ordinary. At the county fair that year, Doherty and Willis showed their spirit photographs, the first exhibit of its kind at an agricultural fair, at least as far as the *Weekly Journal* could tell in 1869. After the fair, interest in spirit photographs

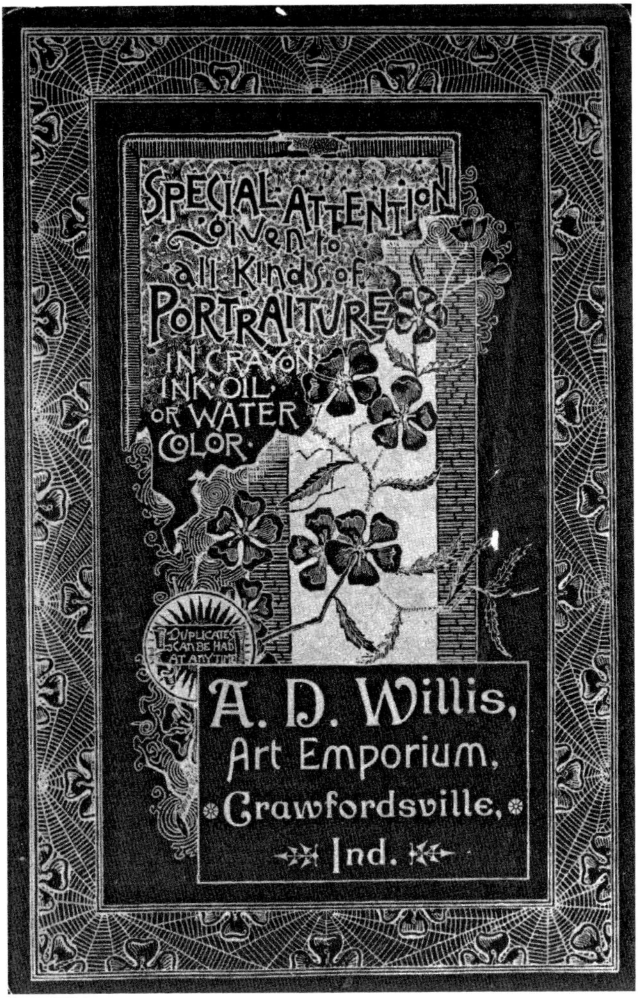

The elaborate back of a cabinet card from the A.D. Willis Art Emporium in Crawfordsville, Indiana. *CDPL Photo.*

skyrocketed in Crawfordsville. Reminders appeared in the *Weekly Review* to "get your spiritual photograph taken" (October 23, 1869). Willis became so popular as a spirit photographer that in 1871 he opened a gallery in Chicago; Fisher Doherty's son, Madison (Matt) Doherty, opened a gallery in Indianapolis in 1871 as well. Spirit photography created excitement in Indianapolis, but the *Weekly Journal* reported on August 24, 1871, "It has got to be an old thing over here."

Spirit photography was taken seriously in some circles as evidence of life after death, but at the same time it was a not-so-serious novelty. When the authenticity of Willis's photographs was challenged, Fisher Doherty rushed to his defense. Investigations were launched; Willis visited S.P. Eversole, a

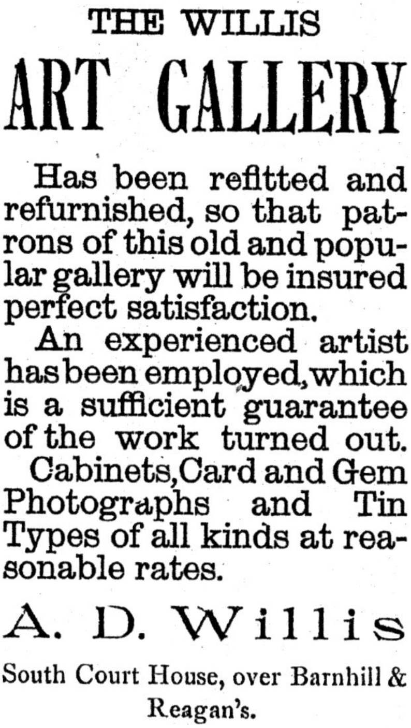
THE WILLIS

ART GALLERY

Has been refitted and refurnished, so that patrons of this old and popular gallery will be insured perfect satisfaction.

An experienced artist has been employed, which is a sufficient guarantee of the work turned out.

Cabinets, Card and Gem Photographs and Tin Types of all kinds at reasonable rates.

A. D. Willis

South Court House, over Barnhill & Reagan's.

A.D. Willis had a long and successful career as a photographer. During the height of the spirit photography craze, Willis opened a gallery in Chicago in addition to his gallery on East Main Street in Crawfordsville. This ad is taken from the *Crawfordsville Weekly Journal* in 1887, after Willis had refitted his gallery and no longer took spirit photographs. *CDPL Photo.*

photographer from Delphi, who could find no trick or fraud in Willis's work. Wiley Kenyon, an educated artist from Crawfordsville (and grandfather of playwright Kenyon Nicholson), theorized that the ghosts were the result of double exposure, but he could find no evidence to support his hypothesis. A Chicago artist of good reputation, Frank Pickerell, watched Willis from sitting to developing and couldn't figure out how it was being done. A letter from J.W. Byrkett of Toledo, Ohio, was printed in the *Weekly Review* on January 8, 1870, in which he stated that there was "nothing of fraud or deception that I could discern. Cannot account for the 'spirit picture.'" Fisher Doherty went so far as to publish an ad in an Indianapolis paper betting anyone from $1,000 to $5,000 to detect a trick or fraud in spirit photography. Whether anyone took him up on it is not known.

Spirit photography, and spiritualism in general, declined in popularity after the nineteenth century. The famous Fox sisters confessed to fraud in 1888; the alleged photographs of fairies that Arthur Conan Doyle believed to be authentic were exposed as fakes, and spirit photographers all over the country gave up their methods of manufacturing false spirit photographs. Although Fisher Doherty remained loyal to spiritualism as interest waned, A.D. Willis refitted his gallery and gave up on the spirit world, never having surrendered his secrets. Was he truly a reluctant photographic medium or just a really talented faker? Montgomery County will never know.

The Week Lana Turner Came to Town

Emily Griffin Winfrey

Celebrities have passed through Crawfordsville from time to time, but actress Lana Turner's 1943 visit was uniquely personal. Turner was the wife of Crawfordsville's Stephen Crane. Citizens were not just meeting one of the most successful actresses of the 1940s but also, more remarkably, a member of their extended family! Recently remarried in March after having their 1942 marriage annulled, Crane and Turner arrived in Crawfordsville on the afternoon of Tuesday, October 12, 1943. In between films, Turner had been on a war bond tour and performing on a radio series in New York City before she made a stop to meet her husband's family for the first time. Exhausted from their tour and returning to Hollywood in a matter of days, the couple asked that no social functions be given, as they preferred relaxation and rest while in Crawfordsville. This statement, printed in the *Crawfordsville Journal Review* on the day of their arrival, did not lessen the town's excitement or prevent the Cranes from making a few social visits during their stay.

Throughout the week, Crawfordsville was abuzz with Lana sightings. Teenagers kept vigil for their favorite star outside the Crane family home at 205 West Pike Street. Years later, local resident Mary Early Johnson still remembered waiting outside the house with her autograph book in hand.

Four days before they visited Crawfordsville, actress Lana Turner and her husband, Private Stephen Crane, conversed with Frank Sinatra at the Stork Club in New York on October 8, 1943. *AP Images.*

She also recalled that she wasn't allowed to go into the house. Those waiting outside would send their books in, and Lana would autograph them and send the books back out to her fans. Eventually, Lana and Stephen came outside to get in their car. Lana "did not talk to anyone or shake hands with anyone, but she was very charming and waved." Robert Garner, another teenager who waited outside, remembered climbing onto the front porch and peering in the window to see Lana and Stephen at the dining table.

Some lucky residents who were close with Katheryn Crane, Stephen's mother, were asked to come into the house to meet Lana. Thirteen-year-old Emma Kolpek and her mother were two invited by Mrs. Crane. Emma reported that Mrs. Crane thought she "was the right age to be impressed with an introduction to a movie star. She was right. All my friends were gaga over the prospect of meeting her. She had beautiful, shiny, silver-blonde hair in a pageboy and wore a short-sleeve sweater. I can't remember what she said. I was speechless, but she carried the conversation and tried to make me feel at ease." Only six years old, Tom Siamas was one of the younger admirers who met Lana that week. A neighbor of the Cranes and well liked by Katheryn Crane, Siamas sat on Lana Turner's lap. Siamas remembered Lana, in more star-like behavior, coming out onto the front porch in her lingerie at one point and saying, "Oh, let me go to sleep!" Mary Early Johnson also said that Lana seemed to want seclusion during her stay.

In the following days, Lana and Stephen walked down South Washington Street, stopping by Producers Dairy Bar and the family business, the Stephenson Crane cigar store. Along the route, the couple met with Mayor Thomas Cooksey in his office. George W. "Bill" Horton Jr. remembered that all the kids hanging out at the Crawfordsville Youth Canteen at 116 South Washington Street "rushed out of the Rec Center to see Lana Turner. To our lustful teenage eyes, she was an utterly unbelievably gorgeous doll." In a *Montgomery County Magazine* article from January 2001, John Waye recalled that he decided to stop by Producers Dairy Bar for a milkshake on his way to the recreation center. When he entered the dairy bar, he was startled to see Lana Turner standing in a "car-length white mink coat, and she was just as gorgeous as she was in the rare Technicolor of the early 1940s movies." Lana never looked in the seventeen-year-old's direction, and Waye, admittedly awestruck, did not approach her.

Five years before he married Lana Turner, Joseph Stephen Crane was a senior studying business at Wabash College. This is his senior photo in the 1937 yearbook. Crane was a member of Sigma Chi, Senior Council and Scarlet Masque. Crane was known as Joe in Crawfordsville but chose to be called Stephen when he moved to California. *CDPL Photo.*

A 1937 Wabash College graduate, Stephen Crane was eager to show Lana

Crane brought Turner to his old fraternity house at Wabash College during their stay in Crawfordsville. When they visited the Sigma Chi house on Wabash Avenue, Crane looked around while Turner chatted with student G.W. "Dutch" Freise. The former Sigma Chi building is now the Kane House. *CDPL Photo.*

his former campus. On Thursday, Crane took his wife to the Sigma Chi fraternity house. Crane's fraternity brothers missed their chance, though! There was only one pledge at the house when Stephen and Lana stopped by. G.W. "Dutch" Freise recalled that he was the lone Sigma Chi there to greet the couple "when Steve Crane came rolling up in his big car and Lana got out. Crane came to see his old fraternity house. I visited with Lana, talked to her. I didn't take any pictures, but some of the guys from the other fraternities came out and ogled her. She was a lovely lady and very kind. She was not that much older than I was. Crane didn't say much. He just looked around the house while I talked to Lana."

The couple was impressively dressed for their visit. The recently enlisted Crane, as Bill Kennedy described two days later in the Wabash student paper *The Bachelor*, was "looking very sharp in the most salutable private's uniform I have seen." Lana was noted as looking exactly as she did onscreen and earning the title "Sweetheart of the Sigma Chi." Wabash alumnus Ken Larsen remembered seeing Lana on campus, but Dick Ellis only recalled the elusive search to find her. Excited to meet her, Ellis and his friends "made a number of extra trips to downtown

Crawfordsville in hopes of seeing her," but alas, the glamorous actress was never spotted.

On Thursday evening, Lana dined with Crane's extended family at the Crane residence. The intimate dinner included Stephen's grandmother, Henrietta Stephenson; uncle and aunt, Mr. and Mrs. R.R. Stephenson; and cousin, Alice Stephenson. In *Lana: The Lady, the Legend, the Truth*, Turner recalled Crane's family as "sweet, comfortable, down-to-earth people. They did their best to make me feel at home. But the whole time it was clear that it was not my home. They regarded me as a curiosity, not a member of the family but someone from another world." A month later, in the *Los Angeles Times* of November 7, Turner would remark that the trip to Crawfordsville was "a revelation of family." Before Turner could explain, her husband interjected, "My grandmother is empress of the household. She carries a cane which is expressive of her authority, and there is no greater social error that may be committed in our family than not to greet her first upon your arrival. The entire family expects you to do that." One wonders if Turner committed this great social error upon meeting Crane's family for the first time.

Lana and Stephen's final social call in Crawfordsville was at the County Children's Home at 1605 West Wabash Avenue. According to the October 16, 1943 *Journal Review*, Turner toured the home and answered the children's questions. She treated the children to candy and ice cream, and they presented her with a homemade cake with her name on it. Mary Ann Oaks was able to celebrate her eleventh birthday with the star and received a kiss and money as a gift. In the August 1979 *Montgomery County Magazine*, Jayne Jeffrey remembered that every child was given an assignment for the day and that she was the lucky one who got to hold Lana's mink coat throughout the afternoon. Lana Turner delighted the children when she sat down on the floor and played games with them.

On Saturday, October 16, Stephen Crane and Lana Turner departed Crawfordsville on a train bound for Chicago. Gilbert Custer, then ten years old, remembered seeing Lana Turner at the Monon Station at North Green Street: "Everybody knew she was coming. Everyone surrounded her. They kept a respectable distance, but they just gathered around her. I remember the crowds. You couldn't stir them with a stick!"

Crawfordsville citizens continue to fondly and excitedly recall the visit today, but Turner and Crane's relationship was damaged by it. So eager to give his wife a tour of his hometown, Stephen Crane somehow overlooked that the newspapers' embellishments of his past (and his reluctance to correct them) would come to light on this trip. Unfortunately, Crane's false identification in

Lana Turner did not know her husband's true background until she visited the Stephenson Crane cigar store (pictured as it looks today). Located at 107 South Washington Street, it is now the site of Urban Initiatives. It is distinguished as the Crane Building on an exterior plaque. Stephen Crane managed this store after his father's death in 1935. The store would remain the Crane cigar store until the 1980s. *CDPL Photo.*

Hollywood as a tobacco heir caused him to become a bit of a good-natured joke in his hometown. The people of Crawfordsville knew firsthand that Crane was no heir but rather the son of a downtown cigar merchant and pool hall owner. Lana Turner was not aware of Crane's true background until she came to Crawfordsville. Thirty-nine years later, in her autobiography, Lana Turner would reflect on her discovery of the truth when they visited the Stephenson Crane cigar store. "Stephan [*sic*] stopped the driver at a storefront marked Beer, Tobacco, Pool…It was only then that I realized this was the tobacco business Stephan had mentioned so casually when I first met him… From then on I couldn't help seeing Stephan with different eyes. Why had he felt it necessary to imply he was something he wasn't?"

Turner had already been surprised by her husband once before: early in their marriage, she discovered that Crane was still legally married to his first wife, Carol Ann Kurtz of Indianapolis. Although Crane claimed that it was an honest mistake and that he had believed the divorce was finalized, Turner annulled the marriage. But when Turner discovered that she was pregnant, the couple remarried a little more than a month after their annulment. The trip to Crawfordsville came just three months after the birth of a daughter, Cheryl, following a difficult labor and nearly fatal illness for Turner.

According to the *Journal Review* published on the day of their departure, Turner and Crane expressed their wish to return to Crawfordsville with their daughter in March. They would not return. Less than a year later, the couple divorced. Lana Turner would continue to be a top box office draw throughout the next several decades. Stephen Crane made an attempt at an acting career, but after three films with Columbia Pictures, he turned his attention to the restaurant industry. As a restaurateur of high-profile establishments, Crane was able to gain as much respect as he aged as he had gained notoriety with the embellishments of his youth. Although he never returned with Turner, Crane did return to Crawfordsville for his mother's funeral just three years later in 1946, and he visited friends in his hometown again in the 1950s. Before his 1985 death, Crane chose Crawfordsville as his final resting place, requesting to be buried by his parents' graves at Oak Hill Cemetery. Lana Turner and Stephen Crane would both achieve lasting success in their careers, but neither was as fortunate in their future marriages. Here, the couple will always be remembered as they were in October 1943. For one week in Crawfordsville, they were a young couple, early in their marriage and their careers, and they created an unparalleled excitement that has never been forgotten.

Commodore Alf's Improbable Gourd Museum

Jodie Steelman Wilson

Today, gourds are primarily associated with the Thanksgiving holiday and fall decorations, but in the past they had far more important uses. In the times of early settlers, gourds were considered indispensable crops, providing bowls, drinking cups and other necessary supplies when carved. But it took Alfred Lookabill, Crawfordsville realtor and entrepreneur extraordinaire, to inspire appreciation of the humble gourd among presidents and politicians, drawing many visitors to Crawfordsville in the process.

Lookabill's Gourd Museum came about after the retirement of the Civil War veteran, longtime realtor and farming enthusiast. In about 1897, he began growing gourds on his farm, located two miles west of Crawfordsville, after a friend gave him a dipper gourd for Christmas as a joke. Planting the seeds contained within the gourd rewarded him with a bumper crop of dipper gourds, which he planned to share with his friends. But among the gourds were a few of unusual shape that inspired him. With the encouragement of General Lew Wallace, an occasional visitor to his farm, he began to search for additional varieties of gourds to add to his collection. Soon he had many kinds of gourds, which he learned to grow in molds, carve, paint and otherwise craft in a wide assortment of forms. One source, the *Indianapolis Sunday Star*, claimed in 1924 that the museum contained ten thousand gourd specimens, representing an amazing five hundred varieties of gourds, quite an accomplishment for a venture launched from a gag gift.

After H.R. Tinsley's hardware store at 121–123 South Washington Street displayed the gourd birds crafted by Alf Lookabill, local photographer Thomas B. Nicholson captured this image of the Commodore and his flock. *CDPL Photo.*

According to the *Indianapolis Sunday Star*, although Lookabill had no previous artistic training, he saw the possibilities inherent in the diverse shapes of different gourds, ranging in size from small ones the size of a man's thumb to ones as large as a bushel basket. His creations included musical instruments, such as violins, guitars and horns; useful household items, such as scrubbing cloths, coffeepots, sugar bowls, cups and plates; and sculptural works, including chickens, geese, cats, dogs and even a buffalo head. One of his masterpieces was a three-foot-tall clock created—except for the clock's mechanism and cover—exclusively of gourds. Even the letters on the sign at the Lookabill Gourd Museum were created using gourds.

Lookabill had already demonstrated an unusual talent for self-promotion, which he used to market his real estate business. During his career, he wrote all his advertising copy himself and adopted the nickname Commodore Alf during the Spanish-American War. After his successful career in real

Alfred Lookabill holds a gourd violin, created from a gourd grown in a mold to the correct size and shape. Lookabill's collection included other musical instruments constructed from gourds, including horns and guitars. *CDPL Photo.*

estate ended, he turned his marketing ability and love for agriculture in a successful, although improbable, direction, conceiving the idea of a gourd museum for Crawfordsville. In 1906, Lookabill applied for copyrights for three photographs of his museum and collection, providing himself with illustrations for marketing materials and postcards to be sold to the visitors.

But drawing a crowd to the museum would take some doing. The Commodore was equal to the task, and he set about to reach out to politicians. In the same year, he mailed an example of a new variety of gourd he had developed to President Theodore Roosevelt, calling it the "Roosevelt Gourd" in his honor. In an article appearing in the *Massachusetts Ploughman and New England Journal of Agriculture* in March 1906, the honor was summarized, mentioning that Reverend H. Randel Lookabill, the son of Alf Lookabill, had presented the gift to the president, who was delighted by it. Reverend Lookabill's father, the article noted, was "the greatest gourd raiser in the world."

The *Crawfordsville Daily Journal* reported on May 30, 1907, that ex-president Grover Cleveland had written to Alf Lookabill about his gourds. Lookabill's son, Randel, had visited Cleveland at his estate in Princeton, New Jersey, mentioning that his father was a gourd expert, and had shown Cleveland photographs of the museum. Cleveland expressed his interest in receiving some gourd seeds to grow, and so Commodore Alf had mailed him seeds of several varieties, with his copyrighted photographs of the Gourd Museum,

Above: An interior view of Crawfordsville's Lookabill Gourd Museum shows the extent of the specimens included in the collection. A photograph of President Cleveland, sent by the president himself, is displayed among them in a frame made of gourds. *CDPL Photo.*

Left: Alfred Lookabill stands with Thomas Riley Marshall, Wabash College graduate, Indiana governor and U.S. vice president for eight years under Woodrow Wilson. Marshall was a frequent visitor to Crawfordsville, and in 1923, he even considered moving to Crawfordsville. *CDPL Photo.*

some notes on growing gourds and a photograph of himself. Upon receipt of the items, the ex-president drafted a thank-you letter that said of Lookabill's photograph, "I hope I may be allowed to say that in placid contentment and the appearance of satisfactory relations to Nature, you look the part exceedingly well." In turn, Cleveland enclosed an autographed photograph of himself, which the Commodore placed in a frame made of gourds and added to his collection.

Lookabill's hero, politician William Jennings Bryan, visited the museum on October 20, 1910, according to the *Daily Journal*. About the museum, Bryan said, "It is the most wonderful thing in my experience, considering it as the development of a lost and buried product." He promised to promote the gourd museum in his publication, *The Commoner*, which he did in an article published on December 9, 1910. Thomas Riley Marshall, governor of the state of Indiana and later vice president of the United States, visited the Lookabill Gourd Museum, and Commodore Alf was careful to have many photographs taken of himself and his family with Mr. Marshall, but the date of his visit has been lost.

At an unknown point in the history of the museum, the entire collection was presented to the Town of Russellville, in Putnam County, where Alfred Lookabill was born in a log cabin in 1838. The town gratefully built a structure to house the donated collection and collected admission fees, but after several years, the Commodore returned, packed up all the gourds and took them back to Crawfordsville. An undated article from a Putnam County source summed up the sentiments of the baffled townspeople when it noted, "We are at a loss to quite understand."

In later years, Lookabill said that although he had been offered a substantial amount of money by the Smithsonian Institution, he felt he could not bring himself to part with his collection, as he told the *Crawfordsville Journal*. The British Museum was also mentioned in another article as being in the process of negotiating for the collection, along with other smaller interested parties. Ultimately, Lookabill awarded his prized collection of gourds and some historical relics to Wabash College, where all four of his sons attended. The fate of the collection is not known; perhaps the collection was transferred to museums or perhaps it was destroyed. In any case, Wabash no longer houses the collection the Commodore created. Lookabill died on August 17, 1925, at the Soldiers' Home in Lafayette. The *Journal Review*, in his front-page obituary, noted that death had taken "one of the most colorful and popular men ever known to Crawfordsville."

Campaigning in Crawfordsville

Rebecca McDole

Since its beginning in 1823, when it was the only town between Fort Wayne and Terre Haute, Crawfordsville has been a crossroads for travelers. By 1875, three railroads passed through Crawfordsville—the Big Four, the Vandalia and the Monon—and later came the interurbans, making the city both a way station and a destination for politicians and celebrities on the campaign trail.

Civil War and Civil Rights

In the years following the Civil War, abolitionist and former slave Frederick Douglass had a problem. For twenty-five years, he had dedicated his time and talents to the emancipation of his people. Having reached this goal, Douglass was now faced with an even harder job: promoting the interests of his race. The Fifteenth Amendment was ratified in 1870, giving the right to vote to all men regardless of race, and in 1875, the Civil Rights Bill was enacted, giving equal treatment to all in inns, public conveyances and theaters. By 1876, Frederick Douglass was making good money with speaking engagements, and he was on his way to Crawfordsville to campaign for Benjamin Harrison and Rutherford B. Hayes.

Douglass's train was late. By the time he had finished his dinner and arrived at the "wigwam" (the Republican headquarters in Crawfordsville), it was already 8:00 p.m., and the crowd was restless and huddled together for warmth. Douglass had three speeches under his belt that Monday, October 2, 1876, and his voice was hoarse, but on Saturday, the Republican newspaper, the *Crawfordsville Saturday Evening Journal*, praised his "beautiful diction, his cogent reasoning and his magnetic eloquence." He made an "earnest appeal for his race" and urged voters not to "bring about a 'solid South' for the Democratic party." He closed his speech by reminding his audience that "the people of Indiana had a great duty to perform, and that was to vote for Harrison and Hayes."

The Democratic newspaper, the *Crawfordsville Weekly Review*, reported on October 7 that the speech was not that interesting and may have had the unfortunate consequence of causing Douglass's Republicans to vote the Democratic ticket; the antics of his "little whipper-snapper" body servant, Smith, probably didn't help. The *Crawfordsville Star* claimed that following Douglass's impassioned eloquence, Smith made a "few insane statements; among other things, the remarkable lie that there were no common schools in the South." As it turned out, Frederick Douglass's speaking skills did not impress the citizens of Montgomery County—they voted for Democrat James Williams for governor over Benjamin Harrison, and Indiana voted for Samuel Tilden over Rutherford B. Hayes for president. The results of the presidential election were hotly contested, and Crawfordsville's General Lew Wallace headed the recount in Florida that eventually gave the presidency to Hayes.

Nearly one hundred years later, civil rights still made for a hot-button issue. The year was 1964. President Lyndon B. Johnson signed the Civil Rights Act, and Dr. Martin Luther King Jr. was awarded the Nobel Peace Prize. And on May 3, controversial Alabama governor George C. Wallace visited the Fremont Street Baptist Church in Crawfordsville. Wallace, who just a year earlier had made headlines by blocking the doorway to two black students at the University of Alabama, was notorious for his segregationist views and was running in the Indiana primary for president. Crawfordsville residents did not welcome him with open arms; rather, they wrote an open letter to the *Crawfordsville Journal Review* on May 2, 1964, in which they endorsed the First Amendment right to free speech but found "the difference between Governor Wallace's speeches in Indiana and his actions in Alabama too glaring to go unnoticed."

Wallace's speech was broadcast on a loudspeaker outside the church to the press and an estimated two hundred picketers. He appeared nervous

Fremont Street Baptist Church, located at 1908 Fremont Street, Crawfordsville, pictured with its congregation in front. Alabama governor George C. Wallace spoke here on May 3, 1964, to about five hundred people inside the church, and his speech on communism and western world philosophy was broadcast outside the church as well. Two hundred picketers carried signs that read, "All Men Are Equal," "There Is No Color in Religion" and "Color Is Only Skin Deep." *CDPL Photo.*

and on edge, but his comments on communism, equality and prayer were politely received. Upon exiting the church, the governor shook hands and signed autographs before giving an interview to the Wabash College radio station, and he left for Indianapolis without incident. Wallace's bid for the presidential nomination was unsuccessful; Lyndon Johnson was reelected president in 1964 by a large margin.

KEEPING UP WITH THE ROOSEVELTS

Two of America's most popular and beloved presidents, Theodore Roosevelt and Franklin Roosevelt, stopped by Crawfordsville while campaigning. While Teddy was well known at the time of his visit, Franklin Roosevelt was relatively new to politics and warranted just one small mention in the *Crawfordsville Daily Journal*. Teddy Roosevelt, soldier, hunter, author and former president, caused quite a stir when he arrived on the Big Four from Veedersburg at 9:45 a.m. on October 13, 1910. He had been touring Indiana, and the *New York Times* reported on October 14 that crowds were small and hard to arouse in Indiana. But

Crawfordsville was the first crowd that showed enthusiasm for the man the *Daily Journal* called the "greatest living American."

On Ingalls Field at Wabash College, with Wabash boys acting as guards, the *Daily Journal* also reported that Roosevelt's first words were, "Can't I get the Wabash boys up closer?" Giving the Wabash yell, the boys rushed in a mad stampede; an article on October 22 in the Wabash student newspaper, *The Bachelor*, claimed indignantly that a woman and young child were "somewhat roughly shoved about, to put it mildly." Teddy spoke for about fifteen minutes on Progressive republicanism and driving the special interests out of politics, and he encouraged people to vote for Albert J. Beveridge for Indiana senator. As he left the field to cheers, the Wabash boys threw down their hats for him to walk on.

Due to mechanical trouble on the train, Roosevelt held an informal reception after his speech. He greeted people, shook hands and entertained the younger boys with stories about hunting lions in Africa. His parting shot, repeated in the *Daily Journal*, was that "to fail to reelect Beveridge would be an infamy and that any Republican...who would vote against Beveridge would have to spend the rest of his life explaining why he did so." Republicans had a lot of explaining to do that November—Beveridge lost his Senate seat to John Worth Kern. In fact, every candidate Roosevelt campaigned for was defeated.

Franklin D. Roosevelt's vice presidential campaign visit to Crawfordsville was part of a Democratic Party rally, with party workers and Democrats from all over the county in attendance. The *Daily Journal* called Roosevelt "one of the strongest speakers in the present campaign," and he was extended a hearty greeting when he arrived on the Big Four from Danville, Illinois, on October 13, 1920. He took breakfast at the Crawford Hotel (where the Canine Plaza is now, on the corner of Green and Main Streets) before addressing a crowd on the courthouse steps. He spoke about the League of Nations and the Democratic candidate for president, James Cox. There was debate at the time over whether the United States should join the League, and especially about Article 10, which required members to defend any other member if it were attacked. Roosevelt claimed that he and his running mate supported the League of Nations, but with amendments. Cox and Roosevelt lost the election to Harding and Coolidge; Franklin Roosevelt won the day in the end, though, when he was later elected to an unprecedented four terms in the White House (1933–45).

PRESIDENTS, EX-PRESIDENTS AND WANNABE PRESIDENTS

"The Great Commoner," William Jennings Bryan, was one of the best-known politicians of his time; he ran for president three times and lost all three elections. He was respected in Montgomery County and visited many times, drawing big crowds and enthusiastic applause for his great orations. In 1898, he passed through the city en route from Bloomington, Illinois, to Lafayette, Indiana. After all the applause, handshaking and waving, Bryan was only able to comment on the loyalty of Democrats before his train pulled away.

Over a decade later, Crawfordsville's support of Colonel Bryan was undiminished. A week after the stir caused by Theodore Roosevelt, Bryan arrived in town on October 20, 1910, to talk up his candidate for Indiana senator, John Worth Kern. The *Crawfordsville Daily Journal* reported on his visit the same day. He arrived on the interurban at the Methodist church corner at Wabash and Water Street at 10:30 a.m., and he was taken to the Crawford Hotel. He was given a tour of the city, spending forty-five minutes with Commodore Alf Lookabill at the famous gourd museum. School was cancelled, and both the Crawfordsville Band and the Colored Band played. The crowd was so big at the Airdome Theater at 225 East Main Street that Bryan was forced to speak twice, once to the overflow of people outside and again to the people inside. Mr. A.N. Foley introduced him as "the greatest citizen in public or private life, and the greatest American orator, living or dead." Bryan urged the kids to stay in school before asking them to make room for the grown-ups. He talked party politics, praised his "friend" John Worth Kern and took a shot at Roosevelt's speech in Crawfordsville the previous week. William Jennings Bryan's popularity may have had a positive effect on the election; his candidate won out over Roosevelt's.

Eight years later, the United States was in the midst of World War I. On April 5, 1918, the Third Liberty Loan drive in Crawfordsville was to be officially opened by the guest of honor, ex-president William Howard Taft. Excitement was at an all-time high in the city; the mayor urged everyone to fly patriotic colors and participate in the celebration. The *Daily Journal* printed an itinerary of the day: the festivities started that afternoon with meetings and addresses, followed by a parade at 3:15 p.m. More than 2,300 schoolchildren marched in the parade, and everyone did their patriotic best to show that they were willing to help "swat the Kaiser." The *Daily Journal* also noted on April 6, "As a variation of the usual procedure in such cases, the parade started on time and went off smoothly and with an entire

President William Howard Taft (1909–1913) in April 1918, with John C. Snyder, president of the chamber of commerce and, later, president of the Ben Hur Life Association, in front of Snyder's home at 201 Wallace Avenue. *John Kummings and Mary Kummings.*

absence of any confusion." Taft arrived at 4:40 p.m., was given a reception at the Supreme Tribe of Ben Hur building (which still stands at the corner of Main and Water Street) and had dinner at chamber of commerce president John C. Snyder's home at 201 Wallace Avenue. His speech, titled "The Menace of a Premature Peace," was given to a full house at 7:00 p.m. in the Wabash College gymnasium; he discussed German militarism and German spies in America. Afterward, the Purdue Band played songs such as "Keep the Home Fires Burning," "Over There" and "Liberty Bell." Four Boy Scouts—Joseph Dye, Robert Max Pittman, James Kenon and Gerald Wilhite—were presented medals by the ex-president for their success in selling Liberty bonds. Taft's visit drew what the *Daily Journal* called "one of the largest crowds that ever packed the city."

Less fanfare but tremendous excitement greeted America's thirty-third president on September 17, 1948, as Harry S Truman began his whistle-stop tour for reelection. Speaking from the back of a train, Truman spoke simply and on the issues most important to his audience. In Crawfordsville, those issues were farm and labor. Truman's stop in Crawfordsville was planned for eleven o'clock on the morning of October 12.

MEMORANDUM: Re:	Appearance of President Truman at Crawfordsville, Montgomery County, Indiana, on October 12, 1948.
TIME OF ARRIVAL:	11:00 A. M. (CST)
TIME OF DEPARTURE:	11:10 A. M. (CST)
MEANS OF ARRIVAL:	New York Central (Enroute West)
NAME OF LOCAL CHAIRMAN IN CHARGE:	William Wilson, 813 West Main Street, Crawfordsville, Indiana. Phone No. 271-J.
LOCATION OF APPEARANCE:	The President will speak from the rear platform of the train after the train has stopped at the intersection of Washington Street and the railroad track. This is a large area and adequate room on both sides of the tracks and in the street to accommodate the crowd.
SECURITY:	Washington Street will be blocked both North and South. Security measures will be handled by the Crawfordsville City Police, the Montgomery County Sheriff's office, the Indiana State Police, and Indiana National Guard.
PERSONS LEAVING THE TRAIN:	John A. Watkins, Candidate for Lieutenant Governor Jack O'Grady, Candidate for Congress 6th Congressional District. Frank McHale, Democratic National Committeeman Mrs. Samuel Ralston, Democratic National Vice Committeewoman Ira L. Haymaker, State Chairman John W. Leslie, State Promotional Director Larry Foster, Official Photographer of State Committee Ura Seeger, 6th District Democratic Chairman Mrs. Lawrence Arnsman, 6th District Democratic Vice Chairman James Wright, Reporter Crawfordsville Journal Review
NAMES OF PERSONS TO APPEAR ON PLATFORM AND INTRODUCTIONS:	William Wilson, Montgomery County Democratic Chairman Mrs. Eston Elmore, Montgomery County Democratic Vice Chairman. Mr. Wilson will introduce Jack O'Grady, Candidate for Congress 6th Congressional District, Mr. John A. Watkins, Candidate for Lieutenant Governor. Mr. Watkins will introduce the President.

From the Truman Library's collection of 1948 election campaign documents, this memo from the president's secretary describes Truman's stop in Crawfordsville on October 12, 1948. The second page of the document (not pictured) has a section called "People to Know in Crawfordsville" that includes Mayor Clark Jones, Congressional candidates Jack O'Grady and Mrs. Cecil Harden, candidate for governor Henry Schricker and Judge Noble Johnson. *Indiana: October 12 and 15 folder; Speech File, President's Secretary's Files, Harry S. Truman Papers, Harry S. Truman Presidential Library and Museum.*

President Truman speaking in Crawfordsville from the caboose of a Pullman train on October 12, 1948. Standing next to Truman is Montgomery County Democratic chairman William "Bill" Wilson of 813 West Main Street. The woman seated next to Wilson is probably Montgomery County Democratic vice-chairman Mrs. Eston (Dorothy) Elmore. *CDPL Photo.*

Schools were dismissed for the day, and the crowd had swelled to as many as twelve thousand people by the time Truman's train pulled in thirteen minutes behind schedule at the intersection of South Washington Street and the railroad track. Police and National Guardsmen kept the crowd in check, while the Crawfordsville Band played "Hail to the Chief" and Wabash students sang. The president spoke briefly about the rural electrification program and stated that "[t]he Republican Party…[has] worked against the interest of the farmer and will continue to do so," according to the *Crawfordsville Journal Review* on October 12. He asked voters to return him to the White House "and I won't have a housing problem." When he was finished, the Montgomery County Democratic committee presented Mrs. Truman with a bouquet of red roses, and the audience yelled for a song from the musically trained first daughter, Margaret, who declined.

It was predicted, right up to the last minute, that Truman would lose the election. Predictions were wrong. Truman won the majority of both the popular and electoral votes—he wouldn't be house-hunting for another four years.

THE RACE OF '68

On the campaign trail in 1968, Senator Eugene McCarthy, Senator Robert F. Kennedy and Indiana governor Roger Branigan were vying for the Democratic presidential nomination, and the results of the Indiana primary were crucial. From the end of April until the vote on May 7, there was a whirlwind of campaign activity, and Crawfordsville was right in the path of the storm.

Robert F. Kennedy was a celebrity of sorts, being the brother of a popular president killed in office, as well as a senator and civil rights activist. Excitement was high as Kennedy's plane landed at the Municipal Airport in Crawfordsville, and he was greeted by cheers despite the sudden windstorm and light rain that preceded him. He was taken to Boulevard Mall; the Cambridge Inn, where he was to speak, was packed, much to the annoyance of mall employees who normally ate lunch there. His speech touched on the rising cost of living and the expense of the Vietnam War. After speaking, Kennedy was taken to a local hotel to rest before his next stop that day in Terre Haute.

Senator McCarthy was no stranger to the city; in 1960, he visited Wabash College to address the students there. Before his scheduled visit on May 6, 1968, McCarthy sent a few friends ahead to warm up the crowds. On April 20, Paul Newman stopped by Crawfordsville on McCarthy's behalf, joking with his audience and recalling his football days at Kenyon College (Newman played in the 1942–43 season when Wabash beat Kenyon badly) before turning serious with talk of the coming vote. A week later, actress Myrna Loy was the guest of honor at a reception sponsored by Citizens for McCarthy. Loy was excited to come to Crawfordsville, home of Lew Wallace; her first film was 1925's *Ben-Hur*.

When Senator McCarthy finally made it to Crawfordsville, he spent about an hour here shaking hands and surprising a group of bowlers by climbing aboard their bus before speaking from the steps of the courthouse about the election. He left the city at 3:00 p.m. and stopped in Linden, where he played baseball with a group of children.

On May 8, the results were in: Kennedy, contrary to expectations, won over Indiana voters—but not those in Montgomery County. Governor Branigan received 1,609 votes to Kennedy's 1,306 and McCarthy's 1,262. Just one month later, Montgomery County and the rest of the nation mourned Robert Kennedy after he was shot in the kitchen of a Los Angeles hotel. The presidency ultimately went to Republican Richard Nixon.

Whether the candidate was popular or unknown, Crawfordsville greeted him warmly. (The exception was President Herbert Hoover, whose train passed through town on June 17, 1931. Despite the thousands of people gathered at the crossings, the cheers and clapping were halfhearted.) Although the excitement of the railroad age has subsided, Crawfordsville has a history of being a nerve center in Indiana that attracted the famous and infamous.

Dying to Stay Married

Emily Griffin Winfrey

On March 27, 1896, Reverend Kagle united in marriage John Bowen, a twenty-two-year-old farmer from Bowers Station, and Laura Sikes, a nineteen-year-old girl from Yountsville. John Flanagan, brother-in-law of John Bowen, had already signed as a witness when the couple applied for marriage in Montgomery County two days earlier. In the application, Flanagan swears that Bowen and Sikes are both of lawful age and that the parties are not first cousins. Actually, Laura was not yet eighteen at the time, but that was not all. John Bowen's mother, Emily Ann Sikes, and Laura Sikes's father, William Sikes, were siblings, which made the applicants first cousins and Flanagan guilty of perjury.

The young couple managed to keep their elopement a secret, but the *Crawfordsville Daily Journal* reported that within three days of the marriage, an angry William Sikes swore that he would prosecute Flanagan. Several weeks later, Laura's concerned uncle, Sam Sergeant, swore out a warrant for Bowen's arrest on William Sikes's behalf. Cousins marrying illegally was already fodder enough, but what occurred on April 18, 1896, would create sensational headlines not only in Crawfordsville but also in prominent newspapers around the country.

On April 19, 1896, the *Chicago Daily Tribune* reported the melodramatic tale involving a beautiful young bride with a "wild mental condition" who shot herself in front of the Montgomery County Courthouse. The *Tribune* related that a sobbing Laura was roughly pulled away from her husband's embrace as he was led to the jail. In response, Laura rushed out onto South Washington Street, grabbed a revolver from her husband's carriage parked in front of the Otto Jewelry Store (as of this writing the site of Creek Jewelers) and placed it against her chest. Laura's father and uncle hurriedly followed her into the street, and her uncle grabbed her arm as she pulled the trigger. The bullet passed through Laura's arm before hitting her father, and the *Tribune* noted that the injuries were so serious that the parties involved would probably not recover.

A day earlier, on April 18, the *Daily Journal* had more accurately reported the injuries. Although Laura was shot in the arm, the wound was not serious. Her father, William Sikes, was merely scratched by the bullet's contact. Still, the spectacle made quite a scene. Laura was quickly attended to by Dr. Enoch Wood Keegan, former Civil War surgeon and pioneer Crawfordsville doctor, at his office at 109 South Washington Street. As she was being treated by Dr. Keegan, Laura "lay moaning and sobbing while hundreds of curious spectators thronged about outside attempting to get a look at her." According to the local article, Laura agreed to return to her parents' home almost immediately after the ordeal and apparently "did not love John enough to wish to share his incarceration." Because he could not afford the $200 bail, John Bowen remained in jail and helpless to remedy the situation.

Dr. Enoch Wood Keegan attended Laura Sikes Bowen after she shot herself in front of the courthouse. Keegan had been practicing medicine in Crawfordsville since 1862 and had served as county coroner and city councilman. Curious onlookers waited outside as Bowen was treated in Keegan's office at 109 South Washington. *CDPL Photo.*

Bowen did, however, offer his side of the story to the press while he was incarcerated. On April 23, a *Crawfordsville Star* reporter called Bowen an "ignorant uncouth youth" but also "an open-hearted fellow" before Bowen described the courtship of his cousin. Bowen said that the relationship had been opposed by the parents not because of the familial relation but because Laura was underage. Laura's suicide attempt in front of the courthouse had not been the first. When her parents objected to the courtship, Laura attempted to hang herself. To keep their daughter from despondency, Mr. and Mrs. William Sikes consented to the relationship and, later, the engagement. Throughout the interview, Bowen cried and seemed genuinely grief-stricken.

Two days after his arrest, his father, William Bowen, provided bail, and John Bowen was released from jail. On the same day, Laura Sikes's brother collected her belongings from her husband's home, but according to the April 20 edition of the *Daily Journal*, John Bowen was expected to "reclaim his bride." Although early reports noted that Laura's father was distraught over the marriage, both Bowen and William Sikes himself later denied these statements. Bowen blamed his arrest on Laura's uncles, Sam Sergeant and Taylor Sikes, both of whose names are frequently changed and have many alternate spellings throughout the newspaper articles. William Sikes agreed with his son-in-law. Sikes claimed that he held no responsibility for the filed complaint against his daughter's husband and stated that he planned to take both John and Laura to his home. From the reports, it is clear that Sam Sergeant did instigate the arrest and that he thought as negatively about his niece as he did her chosen husband. To the *Daily Journal* on April 18, he stated that Laura had been "perverse and wayward" for some time and that John was a "trifling no account fellow who has no standing whatever. I don't care if he is my nephew, he is no good."

The numerous newspaper articles all vary in detail. With each article involving a different family member's account, the names, dates and narratives are conflicting. However, it is certain that John Bowen did indeed reclaim his bride. Four years following their secret elopement, John Bowen and Laura Sikes Bowen were listed as husband and wife in the 1900 census. Both in their twenties, the couple resided in Sugar Creek Township in Montgomery County, where Bowen farmed. They had an eight-month-old daughter, listed as Blanche M. Bowen (later called May Bowen). According to Montgomery County birth records, John and Laura had two children before Blanche. A male was born in March 1898 but probably died in infancy, as there is no other record of him. A female was born to the couple in December 1896, just nine months after their marriage, but died one month after birth. It is possible that Laura could have been with child when the couple was so publicly separated by family members.

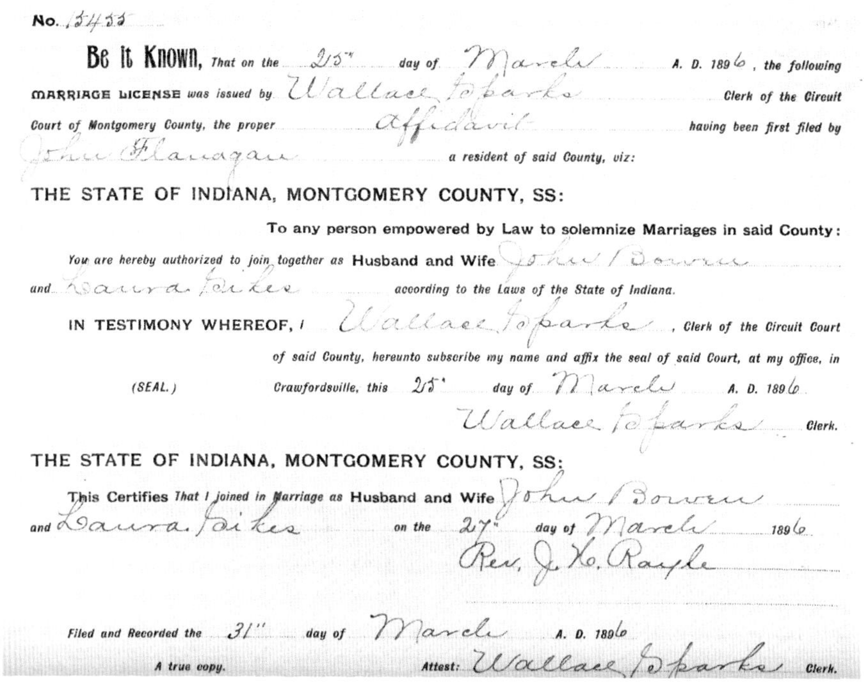

No. 15455

Be It Known, That on the 25th day of March A. D. 1896, the following MARRIAGE LICENSE was issued by Wallace Sparks Clerk of the Circuit Court of Montgomery County, the proper affidavit having been first filed by John Flanagan a resident of said County, viz:

THE STATE OF INDIANA, MONTGOMERY COUNTY, SS:

To any person empowered by Law to solemnize Marriages in said County:

You are hereby authorized to join together as Husband and Wife John Bowen and Laura Sikes according to the Laws of the State of Indiana.

IN TESTIMONY WHEREOF, I Wallace Sparks, Clerk of the Circuit Court of said County, hereunto subscribe my name and affix the seal of said Court, at my office, in

(SEAL.) Crawfordsville, this 25 day of March A. D. 1896

Wallace Sparks Clerk.

THE STATE OF INDIANA, MONTGOMERY COUNTY, SS:

This Certifies That I joined in Marriage as Husband and Wife John Bowen and Laura Sikes on the 27th day of March 1896

Rev. J. H. Rayle

Filed and Recorded the 31st day of March A. D. 1896

A true copy. Attest: Wallace Sparks Clerk.

The marriage certificate of Laura Sikes and John Bowen. The couple was married on March 27, 1896, in Montgomery County after a false affidavit was filed. Sikes was actually underage at the time, and Bowen was her first cousin. Bowen's brother-in-law, John Flanagan, signed as a witness on the false application. *CDPL Photo.*

Despite their early devotion to each other, John and Laura Bowen divorced in 1908 after twelve years of marriage. By 1910, John had married the widow Flora McDaniel (who was neither underage nor his cousin) in Montgomery County. The marriage announcement in the September 17, 1910 *Daily Journal* noted that Bowen and McDaniel were both young and had been married before, but no mention of the sensational event of 1896 was made. Four years later, Bowen would divorce again and relocate to Boone County, where he married Stella Hill in 1919. He and Stella would settle in Clinton County and have three children together.

Laura Sikes Bowen married John Wile on November 7, 1924. The daughter of John and Laura Bowen, May Bowen (who had been listed as Blanche M. in a previous census) was thirty and living with her mother and stepfather in Boone County in the 1930 census. Wile, a hospital trustee, died at the age of eighty-four in 1951. An obituary in the *Crawfordsville Journal Review* dated October 13, 1951, confirms that his wife was the former Laura Bowen but does not mention May. Just three years later, Laura Wile, now age seventy-five and living in Thorntown, died. Her obituary, printed on January 22, 1954, confirms that she was the daughter of William and Arkie Sikes but does not list her first husband. Laura's daughter with John Bowen is listed as May Wile instead of May Bowen. May would live to be seventy-nine. Although she was twenty-five years old when her mother married John Wile, May's obituary, published in the *Journal Review* on April 16, 1979, states that she was a daughter of John Wile and Laura Sikes Wile.

The man Laura could not live without in 1896 is excluded from both Laura and their daughter May's obituaries. John Bowen's whereabouts after 1944 are unknown, and an obituary for him was never printed in the *Journal Review*. The Sikes-Bowen marriage and suicide attempt has been forgotten with time, but in April 1896, the story was reported and read with interest. Although its key players moved apart from each other, the newspapers of the day will forever identify John and Laura as a desperate young couple involved in a tragic love affair.

"Lament of the Fire Laddies"

Rebecca McDole

Since the volunteer fire department formed in Crawfordsville in 1869, a series of unusual and well-loved mascots have kept the boys company. Numerous dogs pitched in when the fire bell rang. Bob, the cat, was "always willing to do his part"; Captain, the monkey, provided endless entertainment; and until his untimely death, Squizzles, the groundhog, had a varied career at the fire department.

Captain was presented to the fire department by Mayor Voris and Councilman Robb in May 1906. The monkey was a "comical little cuss," according to the *Crawfordsville Weekly News Review*. Cap's life was tragically cut short when he "came in contact with the upper and lower jaws of a big dog at the same instant." After lingering a few days, on October 30, 1907, Cap "curled up his toes for the last time." A similar fate met Squizzles in 1904 after just weeks at the firehouse when he met a stray bulldog. This was a particularly hard blow to the firemen; just a month earlier, in July, their pet groundhog, Billie, had skedaddled from his cozy box of dirt when their backs were turned. Reports in the *Crawfordsville Daily Journal* had him "ambling up Dog Leg avenue looking for his shadow" on July 15, 1904.

The most beloved cat in Crawfordsville belonged to the fire department in 1902. The *Daily Journal* reported that Bob was "pampered and petted so much that the men have actually learned to love him," and he was a source of "never failing amusement and solace" to the firefighters. When

Written on the back of this photograph is a note: "'Buddy' Fire dog—Always got on the truck in Crawfordsville. Taken in the late 1800s." Buddy's collar was silver and was fitted with a small, silver lock. *CDPL Photo.*

a down-on-his-luck traveling salesman stopped by the engine house on the morning of July 26, 1902, with a bug exterminator guaranteed to kill fleas, the firemen let him put some on Bob. "Well, he had no sooner put it on than we noticed that Bob was not acting right," a mournful fireman told the *Daily Journal* that afternoon. "Every minute he grew worse and it wasn't five minutes until he rolled over dead." Bob's death sent the men into a tailspin of grief; all of the men, Chief Vance included, were "as melancholy as a farmer with a mortgage to lift in an off wheat year." With a tear in his eye, the fireman concluded that the "old engine house will be a dreary place for a while."

Dogs held a special place in the hearts of the firemen. Bruno, George Markley's Newfoundland, thought that Niagara fire company was "gotten up principally on his account and other dogs have no business there," as the *Crawfordsville Evening Argus* reported on August 8, 1882. He attended business meetings of the company better than any of the men and was always on the scene when he heard a fire alarm. Sadly, in June 1886, Bruno was found poisoned. He was eight years old and weighed 140 pounds. Bruno was succeeded in 1888 by Colonel, a dog who had "more sense than many people," and Jack, a bulldog, in 1889. Jack was a great friend of the horses, Buck and Barney, and stayed with them at the scene of a fire until they were ready to return to the department.

Buddy, a little black terrier, was the cherished mascot of the department in 1904. Owned by Harry Swan, a brick contractor of 506 West Pike Street, Buddy was "almost the same as an attachment to the fire wagon," according to the *Crawfordsville Star* on August 27, 1904. Wherever he was, when Buddy heard the fire bell, he ran. If he was shut in the house, he barked and raced around until he could go. Buddy's last run was on August 25, 1904. At about five o'clock that afternoon, the fire bell sounded the alarm at the home of Buck Toney on Paw-paw Street (now Chestnut Street) in Goosenibble. Buddy was near Central School (which became the old Crawfordsville High School) and started north on Green Street toward the engine house. "With a yelp and a yowl," he joined the team at Pike and Green Street, but while trying to get turned around, Buddy got under one of the horses and received a kick to the head. He was found "upon his back near the gutter with legs as stiff as icicles," according to the *Daily Journal* on August 26, 1904. The fire boys were devastated and gave Buddy a "burial worthy of his place in life."

Buddy's portrait, taken by Nicholson and Sons in the late 1800s, shows the little black terrier perched on a stool, gazing heroically off into the distance, waiting for the fire alarm to sound.

The Legacy of the Jewish Tailor of Crawfordsville

Jodie Steelman Wilson

The family of local tailor Harry Freedman was exemplary for their talent, intelligence, compassion and motivation. The story of how this remarkable family came to be a part of the Montgomery County community is, in itself, quite a tale. Although Harry Freedman spent fifty years of his life in Crawfordsville, he was not a native-born Hoosier. He was born in the Crimea, an occupied territory of Russia, on August 15, 1888. Because of his Jewish heritage, his future there was anything but secure. In 1905, while protesting against the Russian tsarist regime, he was arrested and briefly detained. Upon his release, fellow revolutionaries in the Crimea insisted that he should leave for America at once and sent him to New York with only his tailor's tools: a needle, thread and scissors. He had the name of a contact in New York and the equivalent of one dollar in currency with him for his journey.

According to Freedman's obituary in the *Crawfordsville Journal Review*, he found a job working for a tailor just two days after his arrival in New York. In less than a year, he had moved to Lafayette, Indiana. Soon he had started his own tailor's shop in a small room on North Ninth Street, which his business quickly outgrew. He prospered in his enterprise and married another Jewish Russian immigrant, Sophia Feinstein, in Lafayette in 1909. Their children were born in Lafayette: Lillian in 1910, Beatrice in 1914 and Daniel in 1921.

In 1920, the family moved to Crawfordsville, where Freedman opened a store at 109 North Washington Street. At that time, the only

Harry Freedman in his tailor's shop in Lafayette. He, wife Sophia and their children moved in 1920 to Crawfordsville, where they became actively involved in the community. *Collection of the Freedman family.*

other Jewish families living in Crawfordsville were the Bischof and Tannenbaum families. But business was good for Freedman. And when the Depression took its toll on local workers and their families, Harry Freedman took action to improve conditions for all residents. Daughter Beatrice remembered her father's concern for his fellow man in her autobiography (featured in *Something About the Author*):

> *My father, whom I admired, believed that one must make a contribution to the community; help people achieve a decent standard of living so that they could broaden their lives intellectually and spiritually. Although my father was a businessman—owner of first one, then several clothing stores—his main interest was community organization. He got our town to hire a social worker; to serve free hot lunches to schoolchildren; to build a municipal golf*

course open to everyone (unlike the one at the exclusive country club); he also organized the unemployed for a march on city hall; he did much, much more that we children were not even aware of.

Not everyone seemed to grasp the social activism of the benevolent tailor. In an interview given in 1968, Freedman recalled that local Ku Klux Klan members came to his store, removed their hoods and asked him if he would join their group. Of course, he refused.

He sold his store and retired from business in Crawfordsville in 1955 but continued his community involvement. During his years of community work, Freedman was an organizer of the Community Chest, a source of help for struggling families during the Depression. He was active in the Montgomery County Tuberculosis Association, the Boy Scouts of America, the Montgomery County Chamber of Commerce and the Montgomery

A family gathering of the Feinstein family, likely to celebrate a religious holiday. Seated at the head of the table is Jacob Feinstein, father of Sophia Freedman. Seated next to him is Harry Freedman with son Daniel. Sophia Freedman, Lillian Freedman and Beatrice Freedman are seated next. Although the family was of Jewish heritage, the Freedmans did not give their children a Jewish education and did not participate in organized religious services. *Collection of the Freedman family.*

Despite getting a late start in artistic training, Sophia Freedman had remarkable talent and studied with Fritz Schlemmer. This is her first work of sculpture, a self-portrait. *Collection of the Freedman family.*

Chapter of the American Red Cross. He also was a former president of the Utility Service Board of the Crawfordsville Electric Light and Power Company. After Freedman's death in 1970, the City of Crawfordsville changed the name of Mills Place to Freedman Place in his honor.

While Freedman was motivated to pursue civic duties, his wife, Sophia, backed his efforts. During her years in Crawfordsville, she was active in working with the Girl Scouts and participated in the League of Women Voters. She was a lifelong supporter of the Montgomery County United Fund For You, which grew from the Community Chest project she helped her husband found during the Depression. In addition to community work, in her fifties she began to study art, becoming a talented sculptor and painter despite her late start. She was a student of Fritz Schlemmer, artist in residence at Wabash College, and after the death of her husband, she moved to New York City, where she continued to be active in the arts until her death in 1980.

The Freedmans' eldest daughter, Lillian, was a professional artist who graduated from the University of Chicago, where she met her husband, Abe Goldman, and later studied at the Kansas City Art Institute. Although she left Crawfordsville after high school graduation in 1928, she returned for a few years in the early 1950s with her husband and children to help her father with his clothing store as he neared retirement. Her obituary in the *Washington Post* mentions that she received a master's degree in social work from Catholic University, likely a result of her father's influence, but she worked only briefly as a social worker. Her art career, however, had great longevity. She studied art at American University in Washington, although she considered herself to be self-taught. Her first public art showing was in 1949, held as part of a Society of Washington Artists event. She had many exhibitions of her abstract impressionist paintings in galleries in Washington, D.C.; New York; Texas; and Indiana. In the 1960s, she helped to found the Associated Artists Gallery near Dupont Circle in Washington, D.C. The Associated Artists Gallery and the Franz Bader Gallery hosted exhibitions of her works, and the Bader Gallery represented her for many years. Her work is included in several private collections. She lived in Washington, D.C., until her death in 2009, at ninety-eight years of age.

Prizewinning children's author Beatrice (Freedman) Schenk de Regniers may be the most visible member of Crawfordsville's Freedman family in her hometown; her name is inscribed on a limestone column outside the library, along with other local authors honored by the community. Hundreds pass by each day and are reminded that Montgomery County holds her in high esteem. According to her autobiography in *Something About the Author*, middle child Beatrice had many memories of her childhood in Crawfordsville that she carried with her through her life, providing a foundation for her writing of children's books. She remembered the smell of wet wool mittens drying on the radiator after days playing in the snow near her home at 15 Mills Place. She still recalled her backyard tree house at her home where she used to hide from company. School memories also stayed with her throughout her life. She remembered dancing, crowned by a wreath of silver tinsel and accompanied by Beethoven's Minuet in G, in a Christmas program given at Willson School when she was seven years old. And she never forgot Mr. Burgess, a Crawfordsville High School history teacher she idolized, who had recommended suitable biographies for the inspiration of the budding author.

She had first begun writing at age seven when her grandfather Feinstein presented her with a diary, complete with lock and key, for all her most secret thoughts. At eight, she wrote her first poem. By ninth grade, she was writing features for the Crawfordsville High School newspaper, the *Gold and Blue*, which was sponsored by Mr. Burgess. Her senior year, she was editor in chief, working with her friends to lay out upcoming issues on the family's dining room table.

After she graduated from CHS in 1931, Beatrice attended the University of Chicago and, due to her father's influence, enrolled in the School of Social Service Administration. Social work, however, proved to be a poor fit for her talents and interests. During the World War II era, she joined the United Nations Relief and Rehabilitation Administration, served in Egypt and met her husband, Francis de Regniers, on her travels.

While World War II was underway, she found a job in a publishing house and greatly enjoyed the work. After this job, she stated, it seemed as if her career drifted purposefully toward literary outlets. She became editor of the Scholastic Book Company's Lucky Book Club in 1961 and retired in 1981, but she wrote her own books before work in the morning, on Mondays (her day off) or on vacations. She wrote about fifty books, many of them children's picture books, over the course of her career, plus a play adaptation of her book *Everyone Is Good for Something*, which was produced in March 1986. Her book *May I Bring a Friend?* with illustrations by Beni Montresor, won the Caldecott Award for 1965. Another book, *The Snow Party*, was awarded a gold medal by the Boys Club of America. She collected many additional honors and awards for her books and for her gift for communicating with children. She died in 2000 in Washington, D.C.

The Freedmans' youngest child, Daniel X., followed in the footsteps of his father in his great concern for others. His brilliance must have showed itself at an early age, as his sister Beatrice recalled with pride that he was the only three-year-old allowed to enroll in kindergarten in Crawfordsville. He spent part of his high school career at Lake Forest Academy near Chicago,

Although Beatrice (Freedman) Schenk de Regniers had no children of her own, she felt that her vivid memories of her own childhood spent in Crawfordsville more than adequately qualified her to write children's books. *Collection of the Freedman family.*

although he returned to graduate in 1939 from Crawfordsville High School, where his classmates considered him the "Groucho Marx of CHS."

An obituary published in the *Los Angeles Times* gave much detail about his career. While studying at Harvard, World War II began, and Daniel joined the army. After suffering a back injury that disqualified him for the infantry,

Dr. Daniel Xander Freedman and his wife, Mary (Neidigh) Freedman. Dr. Freedman spent his career advancing the science and practice of psychiatry and was a professor of psychiatry and pharmacology at UCLA's School of Medicine at the time of his death. *Collection of the Freedman family.*

he volunteered to work with the soldiers as a military psychologist, during which time he saw firsthand the need for more research on brain injuries and their effects. After the war was over, he finished his degree, graduating in 1947. He received his MD from Yale University and then did postdoctoral work at the Western New England Psychoanalytic Institute. He became a professor of psychiatry at Yale and began to study how hallucinogenic substances affected neurotransmitters in the brain. He published more than two hundred journal articles and more than fifteen books during his acclaimed career, and he received many national and international awards. He served as the president of the American Psychiatric Association and was chief editor of the American Medical Association's *Archives of General Psychology*. He died in 1993 in Los Angeles.

Although the Jewish tailor from Crimea doesn't share the same background of many of our Crawfordsville residents, his presence in our town has had great and lasting impact. His contributions and that of his family, both to our local community and far beyond the borders of Montgomery County, are deserving of the local memorials that remain a part of Crawfordsville today, such as the naming of Freedman Place and stone block in the library's wall that memorializes author Beatrice Schenk de Regniers. The Community Chest program also remains as an active legacy in Crawfordsville today, continuing to help families as a source of emergency funds many years after the death of Harry Freedman.

Maurine Watkins Makes Satire Out of Murder

Emily Griffin Winfrey

Maurine Dallas Watkins's *Chicago* character Roxie Hart is based on real-life suspected murderess Beulah Annan. Before writing her hit play, Watkins covered the high-profile trial of Beulah Annan for the *Chicago Tribune*. In 1924, Beulah Annan (who was married to Albert Annan) confessed to shooting and killing her boyfriend, Harry Kalstedt. After changing her story several times, Annan was acquitted of the murder charge. It is clear that Watkins based her own satirical play on Annan's story. But where did the character's name, Roxie Hart, come from?

Watkins was likely influenced to name her main character after witnessing Crawfordsville's own high-profile murder trial in 1914. On October 24, 1913, farmer Walter Runyan shot and killed Arlie Stull, a 1911 graduate of Crawfordsville High School. Maurine Watkins was a Crawfordsville High School senior and former schoolmate of Stull's at the time of the murder and subsequent trial. Although Runyan was eventually acquitted, the trial made the front page of the *Crawfordsville Daily Journal* every day for nearly two months.

Waynetown citizens were shocked that twenty-eight-year-old Waynetown Baptist Church member Runyan, a respected farmer and Republican representative, would murder fellow member Arlie Stull, a popular twenty-one-year-old athlete. After all, the men had been friends for three years and were often seen in each other's company. Known for his physical strength,

Stull worked as Runyan's farmhand as his college schedule allowed. As soon as the murder was publicized, townspeople spoke of the rumor of Stull's parentage. Runyan corroborated that there was a rumor that Arlie was not the legitimate son of John Stull and that Arlie had falsely accused Runyan of starting the gossip. Runyan and those defending him stated that Stull continued to blame and resent Runyan for the rumor. Because of the tension growing between the two friends, Runyan released Stull as a farmhand.

After leaving employment that morning, Stull returned to the Runyan home in the evening. Walter; his wife, Edith; and their son, Byron, were at the dining table when Arlie came to the door and demanded that Walter step outside to "settle the matter," according to the *Daily Journal* on October 25, 1913. After putting on a coat with a gun in its pocket, Runyan and his wife went outside, and Runyan said, "Arlie, be a man, let this thing drop." According to Runyan, this comment set Arlie off. As the young athlete lunged at Runyan, he said, "Be a man? I'll show you I am a man." Runyan stated that he knew how strong Arlie was and feared for his life. In self-

Arlie Stull (pictured here two years before his death) and author Maurine Watkins both attended Crawfordsville High School in 1911. When Watkins was a senior in October 1913, Stull was shot and killed by his friend Walter Runyan. Stull worked as a farmhand on Runyan's farm, and the two men attended church together. *CDPL Photo.*

defense, Walter Runyan shot his friend three times. Arlie Stull was killed instantly. Never denying what had taken place, Runyan turned himself in for the murder within an hour of the crime.

Although Runyan's trial filled conversation, residents respected Walter Runyan and did not want to blame him, according to the *Daily Journal*, "until the affair has been fully threshed out. On the other hand few could be found who wished to assume the attitude of sanctioning the killing of the well-known young man on the grounds of self defense." Nearly two months after the shooting, the trial began. The trial was unprecedented in Montgomery County, and the crowds were the largest on record.

The case grew even more infamous when Samuel Hayes, an important witness who was present for one of Stull and Runyan's final conversations, died on January 13, 1914, the first day of the trial. Preparing to board the train for Crawfordsville to attend the trial, Samuel Hayes fled from the depot as a nearby home caught fire. Running to assist with the fire, Hayes had a fatal heart attack. Whatever knowledge of the murder Hayes had was buried with him. A postcard sent from Waynetown to Bettie Groves, in Daytona, Florida, and postmarked January 19, 1914, shows the effect the trial had on local citizens: "Your Pa said he was sending you the *Review* so you are keeping posted on events here. Last week was a stunner. The trial, fire and sudden death all together about took all the starch out of us."

The rumor about Arlie Stull's parentage was expected to be discussed, but a bombshell was dropped when a second point of contention between the two friends came to light. Apparently, Stull had also been disturbed about a relationship between his married friend and a woman who was not his wife. Runyan admitted that Stull placed an incriminating letter in Runyan's coat pocket for Runyan's wife, Edith, to discover. The letter was written by twenty-two-year-old Roxie Hart, a Waynetown native and second cousin of

Roxie On Witness Stand
To Protect Her Character

Twenty-two-year-old Roxie Hart took the stand on February 4, 1914. Local newspapers reported the alleged relationship between Runyan and Hart, and when Hart volunteered to take the witness stand, the trial seemed to focus more on her than Stull's murder. Hart referred to her correspondence with Runyan as a mere flirtation and was praised for her conduct during the sensational trial. *CDPL Photo.*

Edith Runyan. Roxie Hart made headlines as she took the stand to defend her correspondence and relationship with Mr. Runyan. The sensationalized trial (the *Daily Journal* reported a crowd of five hundred being turned away at the courtroom door on one day alone) certainly would have been followed by Miss Watkins, local teenager and budding writer and reporter.

Because the prosecution used Arlie's knowledge of the affair as a motive for his killing, testimony revolved around Hart's visits, letters and, especially, her physical attributes. Montgomery County's obsession with Roxie Hart grew even stronger when Hart voluntarily testified in order to defend her character. Nine days after the jury was selected, Hart's photo appeared in the paper. Two days later, on January 30, the young woman who had been dubbed a "magnet" entered the courtroom with her father. Wearing a veil, Hart's "almost perfect features" still managed to have an effect. The room fell silent.

Now residing in Centralia, Illinois, Hart stayed at the Crawford Hotel (located at the corner of Main and Green Streets) and continued to attend the trial until she was called to testify on February 4. Deemed the "best witness" by far, the media praised Hart for her collected and confident demeanor and frank, straightforward responses. She admitted that she and Walter Runyan had written letters, visited each other and kissed on occasion but asserted that nothing criminal had occurred. Hart referred to the relationship as a flirtation but publicly apologized for hurting her cousin, Edith.

The jury was not convinced that Runyan would murder his friend Stull just to keep the Hart flirtation under wraps. After all, the affair had ended two years earlier, and many of the witnesses testified that Runyan had told them about Hart. Arlie Stull had forced Walter to confess to his wife and her family, but Walter was forgiven by all informed, and the Runyan household returned to normal. After six weeks of testimony, Runyan was found not guilty of the murder charge.

Some reports focused as much on Roxie Hart's appearance and behavior as they did on the actual details of the crime. The *Daily Journal* of February 4, 1914, described her "luxury of black hair" and how her "large, dark eyes sparkle like coals of fire." The *Crawfordsville Review* also noted Roxie Hart's beauty in detail:

> *Miss Hart is becomingly attired in a blue messaline dress, fur trimmed around the yoke...Miss Hart has a small, graceful figure and is of that striking Italian type of beauty so rare in the western world. She has dark appealing eyes and a clear olive skin through which the crimson tints show when blushes are needful to the setting. When sworn...she made a striking figure.*

The only known portrait of Roxie Hart is this poor newspaper photograph that does little justice to her reported beauty. Hart's attractiveness was described in detail throughout the Runyan trial. Hart was originally a Montgomery County native but lived in Centralia, Illinois, at the time of the trial. *CDPL Photo.*

Thirteen years later, Watkins echoed similar attributes in her character description of *Chicago*'s Roxie Hart as "the prettiest woman ever charged with murder in Chicago." In Act 3, Watkins wrote that during the trial, the judge and jury "feast their eyes on a fairer object...Roxie. And who can blame them?" Watkins described Roxie Hart's hair as "an aureole in the sunlight. Her cheeks are a petal pink, her parted lips a rose." In the play's prologue, Watkins provided an introduction of Roxie:

> *She is slender, beautifully slender...And the face is beautiful, too, with short upper lip, pouting mouth, tiptilted nose, wide dark eyes, skin of the finest texture, and hair the color of flame. Turned now in profile there's a hint of a Raphael angel.*

The characters and plot of *Chicago* are based on trials that Watkins covered for the *Chicago Tribune*, but it is interesting that the former resident should use the name of such a scandalous figure in the criminal past of Montgomery County. Certainly, the Roxie Hart of the local Runyan trial and the sensationalized journalism that followed her must have had an impact on the then seventeen-year-old Maurine Watkins. Watkins would leave Crawfordsville to attend college and work as a reporter in Chicago. Following the success of her play, Watkins wrote successful screenplays in the 1930s. However, by the 1940s, Watkins had faded into obscurity.

Maurine Watkins in a photo from the 1914 Crawfordsville High School yearbook. Watkins was a high school senior when the trial took place. In high school, Watkins already showed interest in writing and theater. She acted in several Crawfordsville High School plays and had her second-prize story published in the school annual. Watkins's play *Chicago* would be published thirteen years later. *CDPL Photo.*

After the Runyan trial, Montgomery County's Roxie Hart lived with her parents, Ambrose and Nina Hart, in Centralia, Illinois. By 1920, the twenty-eight-year-old married forty-four-year-old Russian-born merchant Morris Weisman. Roxie Hart Weisman died in Florida in 1978, just nine years after Watkins died there in August 1969. Three years before Roxie Hart Weisman's death, Bob Fosse and Fred Ebb would revamp Watkins's original satirical play into an award-winning musical play (later a film). Maurine Dallas Watkins's Roxie Hart remains a celebrated character on Broadway today.

America's First Airmail

Rebecca McDole

The morning of August 16, 1859, dawned most auspiciously, clear and bright and "delightful, though the effects of solar were evident in the wilted countenances of our Hoosier sons and daughters." These sons and daughters, noted the *Lafayette Daily Courier*, from nearly every portion of Northwestern Indiana and Eastern Illinois and representing the largest gathering the city of Lafayette had seen were on hand to witness the "Grand Balloon Ascension" of aeronaut John Wise. Excitement was high—maybe too high, in fact. The *Daily Courier* reported the next day that it had never seen so many men so "stupidly and disgustingly drunk." Regardless of the debauchery, Mr. Wise was greeted warmly, and the crowd marched in good order to the gasworks to watch the inflation of the Jupiter airmail balloon.

"Like some newly created planet impatient to take its place in the ethereal universe," the balloon assumed shape, as reported by the *Daily Courier* on August 16 after the excitement had died down. At about 2:30 p.m., Jupiter was ready for flight, and with Wise ensconced in the basket, it was conveyed to the corner of Main Street, where the day's festivities hit the first wrong note. The removal of telegraph wires had been neglected, forcing Wise to bring the balloon up and over. This maneuver caused a rope to slip, and at the prospect of crashing into the side of Lahr's Hotel, the aeronaut decided to land the balloon on the outskirts of the city and then tow it back to the city square.

The Jupiter airmail balloon on its first (failed) ascension from Lafayette on August 16, 1859. The photograph was commissioned by a New York paper and was taken by Lafayette daguerreotype artist J.D. Crane. The audience was requested to stand still for two minutes at the conclusion of Mr. Wise's address while the picture was taken. *CDPL Photo.*

The ballast was taken aboard (consisting of sandbags, food and artesian well water), as well as a beautiful barometer and thermometer and—the reason for the whole trip—a bag of U.S. mail. This was to be the nation's first airmail, and citizens who wanted to send letters to the East Coast were urged by the *Daily Courier* to bring them to the post office by noon on August 16, "properly stamped and directed 'via Balloon.'" The stage was set for Wise to ascend to the heavens. His remarks (which he was compelled to make a public apology for the next day after he expressed his displeasure with the telegraph wire incident) were brief, and his audience, warned beforehand to remain still when he was finished, was photographed by local artist J.D. Crane as the balloon rose. But Jupiter didn't go far. The "ascending power of the balloon had been too much exhausted to overcome stubborn gravity," and it was effectively grounded. Mr. Wise stepped from the balloon in despair, promising another attempt the next day.

John Wise, from his book *A System of Aeronautics*, written in 1850. *CDPL Photo.*

Wednesday afternoon, August 17, was devoid of ceremony, but a crowd gathered at the gasworks and sent Mr. Wise off with "loud and long continued cheers." The balloon rose gracefully without incident and hovered above the city for about two hours before it drifted out of sight southwest of Lafayette.

Mr. Wise's account of his trip from Lafayette was printed in the *New York Times* on August 25, 1859. "The Wabash…presented the appearance of a crooked thread of water. I feel rejoiced—invigorated—extremely happy!" After throwing off nearly fifty pounds of sand and hearing shouts and wood chopping below, Wise decided to descend about sixteen miles south of Lafayette "in the midst of the Grand Prairie" (New Richmond) and investigate. He floated above the ground for about twenty minutes, sharing his bread and handing out newspapers, and then ascended again, waving the American flag to the delight of his prairie audience.

Despite reports sent to the *Lafayette Weekly Argus* that the Jupiter had been sighted at Indianapolis and Columbus, Ohio, Wise was unable to find a suitable current to take him to the eastern seaboard and came down near Crawfordsville almost five hours after he took off from Lafayette. Intending to make a grand entrance in the center of town, Wise unintentionally passed right by and landed five miles from town on the farm of the widow Benefiel. The *Lafayette Daily Courier* reported on August 18 that Wise threw a rope to

The Benefiel homestead. Mr. Wise intended to make a grand landing in Crawfordsville, but when his original plans failed, he accidentally landed here, five miles from town. *CDPL Photo.*

a nearby Irishman, who was too frightened to help, but was finally able to persuade a group of women to tow him in. The *Crawfordsville Review* reported that a number of citizens, seeing the balloon descend rapidly, immediately set off in buggies to lend a hand.

Wise was escorted into Crawfordsville by Dr. T.W. Fry and was greeted at the Crane House (an early Crawfordsville hotel) with three hearty cheers. During his stay, Wise outlined to the *Review* his plan to have "in the course of another year…a regular line of air-ships between New York and St. Louis and if our citizens would subscribe stock to the amount of $50,000, he would guarantee that Crawfordsville should be one of the principal stations." Thinking it a good investment, people were quick to buy stock—"Paul Knapper is reported to have taken five hundred dollars worth." Unfortunately, the Civil War interrupted Wise's plans, and the line of airships remained a dream. Blaming the failure of Jupiter's flight on the poor quality of gas furnished to the balloon by the Lafayette Gas Works, Wise still delivered the 123 letters to the post office in Crawfordsville, where they were put on a train and sent east, making the nation's first airmail a relative success.

John Wise had never seen a balloon ascension when he devised a plan to build a balloon in 1835. Despite his lack of practical knowledge, Wise took off in his homemade hot air balloon later that year, and his career took

A commemorative stamp was issued in 1959 to mark the occasion of the nation's first airmail. This pin reproduces the stamp as it was released. *CDPL Photo.*

off, too. The trip from Lafayette to Crawfordsville was his 232nd flight, and he would make more than 500 aerial trips in his lifetime. In 1879, Wise took St. Louis bank teller George Burr on an excursion in the balloon Pathfinder. Days passed with no word, and papers speculated that it was either a masterful publicity hoax or a heartbreaking tragedy. It was the latter. Assumed to have gone down over Lake Michigan, Wise and Burr were presumed dead. Although Burr's body was eventually recovered, Wise was never found.

One hundred years after the flight of the Jupiter, the United States Postal Service commemorated the occasion of the first airmail with a stamp released on August 17, 1959. The anniversary was a holiday in Lafayette and was celebrated with a symbolic flight in another balloon, Jupiter Jr. Flown by Donald Piccard, son of world-famous Swiss balloonist Jean Piccard (the inspiration for *Star Trek*'s Jean-Luc Picard), the mail balloon flopped again, according to the *Chicago Tribune* on August 18, 1959. After a flight of four miles northeast, Piccard was blown into some trees and had to be rescued by state police. But just as it was a hundred years before, the mail was delivered.

Nellie Coutant, Forgotten Photographer

Jodie Steelman Wilson

For many years after its invention in the nineteenth century, photography was not considered an art form or even a serious competitor to painting and drawing. However, by the turn of the century, photography had come into its own; many professionals and amateurs alike became interested in developing this newest art. The pictorialist movement of photography idealized photographs as artworks for their own sakes rather than as mere reproductions of reality. Alfred Stieglitz, Edward Steichen and Myra Albert Wiggins are just some of the famous photographers who began their careers as pictorialists and are well represented in major museums. And for a brief time, a young Crawfordsville woman with a distinctive photographic style found her place among them.

Nellie Coutant, of 705 South Water Street in Crawfordsville, was certainly a talented amateur photographer. She participated successfully in national and even international photographic competitions with other contestants whose names are familiar today to photography enthusiasts. Coutant's achievements were establishing her reputation, too. In a 1904 article published in *American Amateur Photographer* magazine, a photography critic even referred to Coutant's work as "too well known to be specially discussed"—as if all readers were acquainted with her photography. But this Crawfordsville resident never attained a secure fame, and when she died in 1953, her career as a photographer was not even mentioned in her obituary. In the 1980s, when a scholar contacted the Montgomery County Historical Society for information about Coutant and her career, the society responded by saying that no one locally was even aware that she had ever had any fame outside Crawfordsville. It appeared that a few photographs in the collection of the Crawfordsville District Public Library, some entries in the Crawfordsville city directory and a few (already discovered) basic biographical facts were all that was left of her life.

Although there was interest in further investigating her career, the trail was cold. In fact, there would be nothing further to say if the family of Sallie (Remley) Herr, a frequent photographic subject of Nellie Coutant's, had not stepped forward. For years, Coutant served as photographer for the Remley family. With additional photographs and information, and after new research, far more detail has now been discovered about Coutant, her life and her long-forgotten career.

According to her death record, she was born Christiana Helen Coutant on July 27, 1875, in Crawfordsville, the daughter of Dovetail Buggy manager, inventor and one-time Crawfordsville City Council member Chauncey M. Coutant and his wife, Isabella (Groff) Coutant, an 1857 graduate of the Female Seminary in Springfield, Ohio. Mrs. Coutant was also one of the first teachers of the graded schools in Indiana, according to her obituary in the *Crawfordsville Weekly Journal*, published July 28, 1916. When Nellie graduated in 1889, she was named the best scholar of the high school class and received a scholarship from Adrian University in Michigan, although there is no record that she ever attended. She also received an award for not being late or absent during her entire educational career, according to the *Crawfordsville Star* published June 6, 1889.

She would receive more awards than just these during the years that followed. Nellie herself recounted the story of her beginnings in photography in an essay written on hand camera photography for the Bausch and Lomb *Lens Souvenir* in 1903:

> *My first attempts at photography were made merely out of politeness, a friend having presented me with a pocket Kodak with a request that I become "an expert photographer." After using it a few times, a vague idea of making real pictures with the tiny thing entered my mind. At that time I had never seen or heard of a photographic magazine or exhibit, and had received no instruction in any branch of art. In fact, I refused to have anything to do with "painting lessons." The same little bird on the same little bough with the same mass of leaves, which everyone painted, did not appeal to me. So*

the little pocket Kodak opened my eyes to a new and delightful pastime, and my interest grew until I purchased a 5 x 7 hand camera.

Although we do not know exactly when she began her interest in photography, the first reference found of an award given to Nellie Coutant for photography was awarded by *Ladies' Home Journal* in December 1898, when she won ten dollars for a photograph of a girl's room. An example of her early work, one photograph in the library collection, was taken before 1899. A winning photograph in a Kodak contest, entitled "Give Your Grandparents a Kodak for Christmas," depicts Ambrose Remley and Barnet Hoover. It was recently discovered that the man seated in the center of the photograph is Nellie's father, Chauncey Coutant, who died on January 16, 1899.

By 1902, her career was picking up momentum. The *Crawfordsville Weekly Journal* for December 5 of that year bore this headline: "Three Prizes: One Hundred Dollars and Two Kodaks Won by Miss Nellie Coutant for Amateur Photographs." In January 1903, she won another hundred-dollar

This Kodak award-winning photograph was titled "Give Your Grandparents a Kodak for Christmas" and was taken at 701 South Water Street in Crawfordsville. It shows Ambrose Remley (right) and Barnet Hoover (left) with a Kodak camera. The man in the center was recently identified as Chauncey M. Coutant, the father of the photographer, Nellie Coutant. *CDPL Photo.*

Nellie Coutant took first prize in the 1903 Bausch and Lomb Quarter Century Photographic Competition with this photograph of Sallie (Remley) Herr and nephew Walter Remley titled "A Madonna of the Fields." *CDPL Photo.*

prize, this time from the Eastman Progress Competition. The Bausch and Lomb competition in October 1903 set a new high for her career winnings: $150 in gold, roughly the equivalent of $3,800 today, paid for a photograph of Sallie Remley and her nephew, Walter Remley.

With such success already behind her, she had earned the respect of her peers, who selected her for the Salon Committee for the 1904 First American Photographic Salon, held in New York. Writing about Coutant's offerings at the salon, the *Washington Post*'s James Henry Moser praised the photographer's work: "Nellie Coutant, of Crawfordsville, Ind., sends several good things, of which the *Portrait No. 80 C* is like a Munich painting in strength and realism." In March 1905, she displayed seven works as part of the Fifth Chicago Photographic Salon and exhibited two photographs as part of the American Federation of Photographic Societies' Pictorialists of the Central States exhibition in 1905.

Her work "Toward the Setting of the Sun" was selected for inclusion in Photograms of the Year for 1907, prepared by *Photographic Monthly* magazine. She exhibited just one photograph in the Seventh Chicago Photographic Salon in March 1907. At this point in her career, Coutant's national popularity

Nellie Coutant was awarded a ten-dollar prize for this image, published in the *Burr-McIntosh Monthly* in June 1908. The judges commented that "the features of the third prize-winning photograph, entitled, 'Cherries,' taken by Nellie Coutant, are the gracefulness of pose of the figure and the evident knowledge expressed in rendering the photograph." *CDPL Photo.*

began a downward trend. In 1906, eleven references to her works or awards were found in journals and popular magazines, but in 1907, the number found drops to just two. Although she continued her photography, she published

This Coutant work is both her only colorized photograph known to exist and her only magazine cover, published in *Suburban Life* magazine in March 1909. Toward the end of her popular career, Coutant began to concentrate her publications on gardening. *CDPL Photo.*

only a few times per year and took her career in a different direction, writing articles on gardening and providing her own photographic illustrations. No references to awards or publications have been found after 1912.

Perhaps the photographer whom critic Sadakichi Hartmann called "the wooden-shoe pictorialist" was a victim of changing times. The manipulated photographic images Coutant had managed so well became dated as "modern" photographers began to pursue realism rather than an artistic ideal. But it may have been that family obligations or other interests began to crowd her life. Like photography itself, perhaps Nellie had just moved on.

Although she sold many of her photographs locally, very few of them have survived. A sad reality, since these prints provide a priceless look into the lives and times of local families. One prizewinning photograph, "The Goose Picker," was taken of Jennie Davis of South Water Street and illustrates how even city life often had its agricultural aspects in that time period. A poor-quality reproduction of this work survives at UCLA, and two other Coutant originals are among the photographic works at the New York Public Library. No photographs have yet been found of the photographer herself.

The local records are very sketchy when it comes to Coutant's later years. According to city directories, she worked as a clerk at the Supreme Tribe of Ben-Hur, beginning about 1914 and retiring about 1930. After her sister's death in 1929, she sold the family home on South Water Street. According to her obituary, she lived in the Ben Hur Home in Crawfordsville for a short while, moved to Florida for several years and then later moved back to the Ben Hur Home, where she died on February 19, 1953.

The Sad End of Comedian Ferris Hartman

Emily Griffin Winfrey

On September 1, 1931, a crowd of three thousand people attended a benefit performance that included the best talent in San Francisco followed by a film premiere. The show sold out quickly, and hundreds were turned away. The proceeds of the performance were to aid an ailing famous comedian who had been found weak and without money just ten days before. It was expected that enough money would be raised to "care for him in comfort for the balance of his life," according to the *San Jose News* on August 25. Sadly, the benefit came too late. Beloved actor and comedian Ferris Hartman died one day before the event was to take place.

On September 2, the *Los Angeles Times* explained the impact that Hartman had on his audience and how the same determination to please his audience had resulted in his tragic death. Hartman was noted as an artist who had "done so much to brighten the world around him" and whose pride would "not allow him to seek any favors from the public except through the exercise of his art." Indeed, it was reported that when Hartman was found alone and starving in his hotel room, he explained that he was "waiting on an engagement." On the same date, the *Crawfordsville Daily Journal* ran on its front page the story and Hartman's obituary as first printed by the Associated Press. At the end of the AP obituary, the *Journal* added an important detail for local readers: "Ferris Hartman is a step-brother of Kent Wise and Mrs. Mary Cotton,

Jones Avenue. He was born here and grew up here before going on the stage. His father was David W. Hartman."

Born in Crawfordsville on June 12, 1862, Hartman may have inherited his pride and strong work ethic from his father and grandfathers, all of whom were respected businessmen in the county. Ferris's father, David, was township trustee, and his paternal grandfather, William, a general store merchant, was noted for his strict business integrity. Hartman's maternal grandfather, I.F. Wade, was the first newspaper publisher in Crawfordsville, producing the first edition of the *Crawfordsville Record* in 1831. After selling the newspaper in 1836, Wade owned and managed a tombstone company in downtown Crawfordsville until his death.

The 1870 census places Ferris Hartman and his family in Crawfordsville's Ward 3 and notes that Hartman attends the local school. In 1871, when Ferris Hartman was just eight years old, his mother, Julia, died. Ferris and his younger sister, Alethea Lee, would be adopted by their mother's sister, Sarah Wade, and her husband, A.P. Luse. In an interview, Alethea, who would become an actress and playwright under the alternately spelled last name Luce, explained that she and Ferris were sent to relatives "according to a promise made" between their father and deceased mother. Alethea attributed the careers of her brother and herself to their father, according to the *Crawfordsville Daily Argus News* of September 6, 1895: "You see papa used to take part in home talent entertainments here in Crawfordsville years ago, long before I was born and so it's in the family I suppose to want to act." Strangely, only Alethea is cited in the Luses' obituaries, but both children are proudly accounted for in the obituary of their father, David W. Hartman. According to the *Crawfordsville Sunday Star*, both Ferris and Alethea were performing in separate productions in London at the time of their father's death in 1898.

Hartman studied in Champaign, Illinois, before embarking on a stage career in New York with the Conreid Opera Company in 1885. Over the next thirteen years, Hartman would find success, much of his career being spent as a headliner at the Tivoli Opera House in San Francisco. Despite his success, he still made time to visit his local relatives. The *Daily Argus News* reported that Hartman made a trip back home on November 11, 1889. On May 6, 1895, the *San Francisco Call* profiled Hartman, whom they referred to as an "excruciatingly funny" comedian, a student of his craft and a "big, overgrown collegiate, brimful of wit and humor" in his private life. In 1898, Hartman, now a popular star on the comic and burlesque opera scene, signed a five-year contract to star as a straight comedian after investing his savings to secure the rights to play the lead in *The Purser*, according to the

Already a star of the vaudeville stage, Ferris Hartman invested and performed in *The Purser* in 1898. Although critics praised the play, audiences did not embrace Hartman in the new role. A king of comebacks, Hartman successfully returned to directing and starring in comic operas. *Library of Congress.*

San Francisco Call of March 22, 1898. *The Purser* was a critical success but a commercial failure, and it cost Hartman thousands of dollars.

Quickly returning to other plays, thirty-seven-year-old Hartman began to suffer from the paralysis of his lower limbs and was unable to perform. The misfortune-riddled actor, known affectionately by his peers as "Teddy," was found destitute and ill in New York in the summer of 1899. A fellow performer set Hartman up at a Long Island resort, while San Francisco actors banded together to fundraise for his recovery, according to the *San Francisco Call* on August 10, 1899. In the press, Hartman would always be lauded as one of the most generous and charitable actors in the business. He was known for supporting charities that assisted fellow actors who needed medical or financial assistance, and his friends were only too eager to do the same for him.

By the end of the year, Hartman, appearing "the picture of health and ready money," returned to the Tivoli Opera House and San Francisco. But after several prosperous years as a stage manager and actor at the Tivoli, Hartman abruptly quit in 1905 and embraced a surprising new career as the owner of a cocktail emporium. Mixing drinks behind the bar, Hartman announced that he had no plans to return to the stage, reported the *San Francisco Call* on June 14, 1905. By the next year, Hartman had returned to the stage but was forced to make a quick exit when the infamous earthquake struck San Francisco on April 18, 1906. A widely spread but unsubstantiated legend claims that Hartman and friend, music conductor Paul Steindorff, abandoned the burning San Francisco in a hearse. According to the tale, Steindorff drove the hearse as Hartman sat beside a coffin to gain entry into Oakland, where the military was heavily monitoring access due to the overflow of earthquake refugees. Immediately after the devastating earthquake, Hartman began performing at Oakland's Idora Park, but his venture into the bar business had depleted his funds. Hartman was so poor that a judge lowered his alimony payments to ex-wife Mary, whom he had divorced in 1903, from $100 to a mere $25 per month, as noted by the July 28, 1906 *San Francisco Call*. After his death, Joseph M. Cumming, former bank teller, would talk of Hartman's immense savings account and was certain that "any poverty he suffered was due to business reverses and not any improvidence on his part," according to the *San Francisco Chronicle* on September 1, 1931.

Although he may have been unreliable with his investments, Ferris Hartman consistently managed to make significant and warmly welcomed comebacks to the theater. When the actor returned to San Francisco to perform in *The Idol's Eye* in 1908 after being planted in Oakland for two years, the excited crowd implored him to give speeches between each act of the show, noted the *San Francisco Call* on August 18, 1908. Ten years earlier, Hartman, with his sister Alethea, had attended a show at the Tivoli. Other patrons spotted him in the audience, and the applause grew so loud that the stage performance had to be paused so that Hartman could make a speech, according to the *Call* of April 21, 1898. In an age before mass media, the respected actor's personal plights and professional triumphs always managed to make newspaper headlines across the country. Whether the Ferris Hartman company was out on the field for another baseball game (his stage team would compete against other theater casts) or preparing a new season of comic opera, readers cared about projects associated with Hartman's name, and reporters genuinely rooted for Hartman's success.

The 1906 earthquake (which destroyed many of the playhouses of his youth) and the start of the motion picture industry forced Hartman to reevaluate the future of his career. By 1911, Hartman had created and incorporated the Ferris

Comedian Ferris Hartman in 1909, the year he was described as a "brave pioneer" by *Los Angeles Times* reporter Julian Johnson. *University of Washington Libraries, Special Collections, UW29886.*

Hartman Enterprises Company, capitalized at $50,000, reported the September 14, 1911 *San Francisco Call.* Along with playing to packed houses in California, the company spent several years traveling and performing in the Orient. Many of the performances starred Hartman and his wife, Josephine, but several noted silent film stars also had roles with the company. Both Roscoe "Fatty" Arbuckle and Lon Chaney credited Hartman for supporting their early careers in the entertainment industry.

In a January 28, 1922 interview with the *Evening News* of San Jose, California, Ferris Hartman described his career: "I thought pictures were only a temporary craze—a fad—so I organized a company and went out to the Orient for a year…When we came back pictures were going stronger than ever, so I joined the procession and have been directing screen shows ever since." Hartman produced or directed more than a dozen short films between 1917 and 1921. While Hartman experienced success in the film industry, he made it clear that he longed for his past as a live performer at the Tivoli. In the interview, Hartman openly reminisced about the stars of yesteryear and discussed reopening the destroyed opera house. He wistfully remarked, "Those were the happy days."

Although he was nostalgic, Hartman expressed his pleasure at being viewed realistically in modern productions. "I'm glad to see that the form of light musical entertainment is changing from absurdity to realism. It is now possible for a musical comedian to be a human being, wear honest-to-life clothes and express some semblance of sanity in his lines," he noted in the *Los Angeles Times* on October 31, 1909. As he adapted to changing trends, forty-seven-year-old Hartman maintained the respect of his peers and critics. The *Los Angeles Times* reporter described Hartman in strong terms:

Mr. Hartman is a brave pioneer, and absolutely the only unselfish man I ever knew to embark on musical-comedy seas. Hartman is a fanatic, if you like—at any rate, a man obsessed by one idea: to maintain his company, to hold it, to devote everything but his living to that company, to keep it in shape for the eventual big city that is now marching down the corridor of the future right in our direction...Hartman's company is distinctive and original. It is unique. It is Hartman.

The song "Time Will Cure All Things" was written and composed by Ferris Hartman. Hartman performed this song in *The Purser* in 1898. Hartman's interpretations would make famous many of the songs he performed in his musical operas. *California History Room, California State Library, Sacramento, California.*

Despite his progress and modern accomplishments, Hartman continued to yearn for his former days and made multiple attempts to revive his famous comic operas in the 1920s. These efforts would fail. In between these attempts, Hartman busied himself with speaking engagements, radio programs and local plays. In the spring of 1930, Hartman announced a new season of comic opera at the Shrine Auditorium in Los Angeles. Beginning on June 8, Hartman planned for his company to interpret the works of modern composers. According to the April 27, 1930 *Los Angeles Times*, an enthusiastic Hartman held public auditions and allowed the public to vote by ballots for the songs they desired be included in the production. On May 23, it was reported that technicians were preparing the Shrine Auditorium for Hartman's return to the stage, and on May 28 the auditorium began selling tickets. But the show did not go on. For reasons unknown, the opera was never performed. In October, Hartman was publicly humiliated when the treasurer and a receptionist of his company pressed charges against him for nonpayment of wages. Hartman and partner Lou B. Jacobs pleaded guilty, but their thirty-day prison sentence was suspended on condition that they pay the two employees, noted the *Los Angeles Times* of October 15, 1930.

Less than a year later, Hartman would be found destitute and dying in San Francisco's Dalt Hotel. Even though he was married with five children (including son Hugh from his previous marriage), Hartman was alone and had fainted as he tried to walk to the medicine table in his rented room, according to the *Spokesman-Review* of August 21, 1931. Although friends and fans rallied together quickly to support him, Hartman was unable to make his final curtain call. The benefit that came twenty-four hours too late to save Hartman helped those in similar situations. The performance raised $5,113 and, like many of the charity events that Hartman so frequently supported, went to the aid of unemployed actors.

But Ferris Hartman was not sad as he lay in his bed at St. Francis Hospital in the days before his death. Always enchanted by the spotlight, Hartman was "unusually happy" in the hours leading up to his fatal heart attack. He knew about the upcoming show in his honor and bragged about what he would do as soon as he was back on the stage. Hartman optimistically looked forward to "making the public laugh again" but was realistic about his condition. In his last hours, Hartman asked a friend to make sure that the show would go on no matter his condition because, as he put it, "I'm not the only hungry old man in San Francisco," noted the *San Francisco Chronicle* of September 1, 1931.

Although his life ended tragically, Hartman, a local boy who had entertained audiences across the world, died a happy man knowing that he had not been forgotten. He was proud that his benefit show had sold out and that his name being in the headlines could still elicit adoration among the public. If he had survived, Hartman would have certainly entered the benefit to the deafening applause and standing ovations he had experienced in all his previous comebacks. Instead, fans mourned the loss of their beloved idol of the San Francisco stage and the nostalgia that died with him. But in death, Hartman, smiling in his final moments, was finally able to achieve the recognition he had longed for since the days of his youth.

Crawfordsville's Playwright

Kenyon Nicholson

Rebecca McDole

Crawfordsville is a city that has seen its share of greatness. From Civil War generals to authors (or both at the same time), from actors to inventors and artists, the city has earned its reputation as the Athens of Indiana. From such a rich cultural heritage came playwright John Kenyon Nicholson.

Kenyon's grandfather, John Nicholson Sr., came to Crawfordsville in 1879 after having spent thirty years learning and honing his skills as a photographer. As an artist, John was very successful; he had an ability to capture a natural and lifelike expression, and his business flourished. He taught his sons, John Jr. and Thomas, the art of photography. Thomas was already well known in Crawfordsville by the time he became the sole proprietor of Nicholson and Sons after his father's death in 1893. He was an avid bicyclist and won the Indiana state bicycle riding championship in Terre Haute as a teenager. His marriage to Anna Kenyon in 1893 was celebrated by a large circle of friends. John Kenyon Nicholson was born one year later, on May 21, 1894; his brother, Lawrence Nicholson, was born on May 11, 1896.

Kenyon and Lawrence's childhood mirrored their father's. They were educated in the Crawfordsville schools, attended Center Presbyterian Church and assisted their father in the photography gallery. Kenyon recalled later in life handing his father glass photography plates as Thomas photographed General Lew Wallace beneath his Ben-Hur beech; Kenyon was six years old at the time. Kenyon and Lawrence attended Crawfordsville High School, and each excelled in his own area of interest—Kenyon in drama and literature and Lawrence in athletics.

Here Kenyon's life begins to diverge from his father's. Not content to quietly watch the world through a camera lens, Kenyon wanted bigger things for his life, and he set out to make them happen. On September 7, 1911, he enrolled at the prestigious DeWitt Clinton High School in New York City; his subjects were English, Latin, German, physical training, history and elocution. He lived with his aunt and uncle, William and Bessie (Nicholson) Wheeler, at 61 Hamilton Place, about a block away from the home of Alexander Hamilton and the campus of the City College of New York. He only stayed a year, but his experience with New York's theater life stuck with him when he returned to Crawfordsville to finish high school.

Miss Anna Willson, principal of Crawfordsville High School, nurtured Kenyon's talents. Under her direction, the school put on two or three plays per year and also sponsored open houses in which students would give short performances. In a *Crawfordsville Journal Review* article from May 17, 1972, classmate Lee Detchon recalled a play written by Kenyon for one of these performances, *Coleman's Coterie*. Coleman's Drugstore, located at the corner of the Crawford Hotel, was a popular hangout for teenagers, the place to catch up on gossip. One of the songs was titled, "If a Table at Coleman's Could Talk."

Kenyon entered Wabash College in 1913 and immediately set out to make his mark. He joined the Dramatic Club, the Glee Club and the staff of both student publications, *The Bachelor* and *Wabash Magazine*. The play *Let Him Up, Doc* was written in collaboration with Crawfordsville native Norman E. Tannenbaum, who later changed his name to Norman Treves and became a renowned authority on breast cancer. Performed at the Masonic Temple on December 11, 1913, the show was a hit. Characters like Dr. Cleaver A. Whack and Dr. Hope E. Dyes populated the boys' "musical travesty," and the "Anvil Chorus" brought down the house. Kenyon was elected stage manager of the Dramatic Club in 1915 and continued to write plays and musical comedies.

Writing seems to have occupied much of Kenyon's time at Wabash. His story "Puppets" won the coveted Gene Stratton-Porter award, valued not only for its $100 prize but also because the famous Ms. Stratton-Porter herself was one of the judges. Kenyon told the *Crawfordsville Daily Journal* on June 19, 1915, that the money would stay in the bank as "backing for his future ventures, literary and otherwise." The next year, he was asked to

Wabash College Beta Theta Pi members pictured in front of their fraternity house, circa 1917. Kenyon Nicholson is in the back row, third from left. *Wabash College, Ramsay Archives.*

write a section for the Montgomery County part of the Indiana centennial pageant under the supervision of Professor Hains, pageant master. The section was called "Montamin, a Masque" and represented a legend of primitive Indian days. That same year, 1916, Kenyon was chosen by a vote of twenty-four to two as editor in chief of *Wabash Magazine*. During his years at Wabash, hardly an issue of the magazine appeared that did not include something by Kenyon Nicholson.

Being the big man on campus didn't keep Kenyon from indulging his wanderlust. In summers and on breaks from school, he traveled across America and Europe, filing away stories and experiences to use later in his plays. A story often repeated is that of Kenyon hitching a ride on a chicken truck; in exchange for the ride, he fed and watered the birds. He sailed to Europe as a steerage steward (and published his account of the trip as "Log of a Steerage Steward" in *Wabash Magazine*). He took odd jobs in London and Scotland, including one as a butler, and spent the money he earned to buy a bicycle to ride across France.

The Great War came to Crawfordsville in 1917; by April of that year, over 20 percent of Wabash College had joined up, including Kenyon and his brother, Lawrence. The Nicholson boys went to Officers' Training Camp at

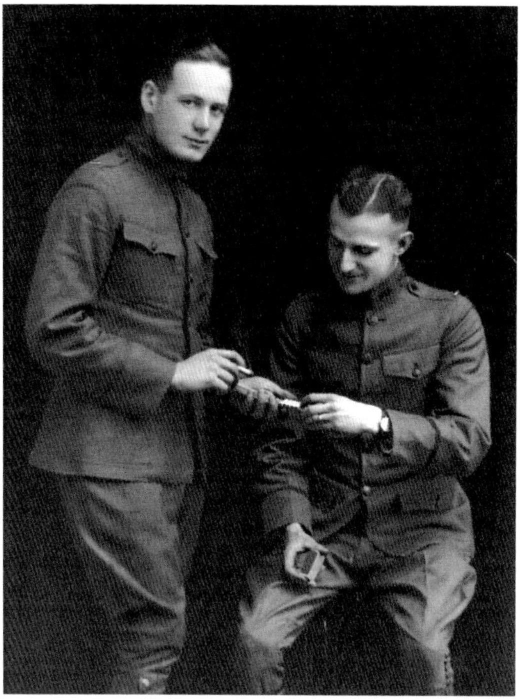

Kenyon Nicholson (left) pictured with fellow Wabash student Marshall Jones in their World War I uniforms about 1917. Kenyon enlisted in April 1917 and served in France for eighteen months as intelligence officer. *Wabash College, Ramsay Archives.*

Fort Benjamin Harrison in Indianapolis and shipped out separately to do their duty for their country. Kenyon got what was considered one of the easiest jobs in the army, that of intelligence officer. He was stationed in France; in 1918, by pure coincidence, he ran into his brother, who had just arrived in the country with another unit. Their reunion was probably short but was a great joy to brothers who had been separated by the war for months.

Kenyon's ambition carried him away from Crawfordsville after the war. He went to Cambridge University in England on Uncle Sam's dime and then came home and took a job as press agent for the Stuart Walker Company, working in offices in Indianapolis, Ohio and New York. He began publishing plays, including *Honor Bright*, written with famed Hoosier author and diplomat Meredith Nicholson (no relation to Kenyon, although he called Meredith "Uncle"). While working for Stuart Walker, Kenyon met the beautiful Lucile Nikolas, an actress with the company. It was a case of love at first sight for both, and they were married on Christmas Eve 1924. From the Stuart Walker Company, the newlywed Nicholsons set out to take on Broadway.

In New York City once again, Kenyon continued writing while teaching drama at Columbia University. His first big success was with *The Barker* in 1927, which had 221 performances between January and July at the Biltmore Theater in New York. He followed this with other, minor successes like *Torch Song* in 1930, *Sailor Beware!* in 1933 and *Swing Your Lady* in 1935. Just as he had worked with other students at Wabash to create his plays, Kenyon rarely wrote solo during his career. He was known as a great collaborator; Kenyon's wife, Lucile, was often an uncredited writing partner. Kenyon expanded his professional repertoire with jobs in Hollywood and writing for radio programs.

Kenyon Nicholson's career roared through the 1920s, glided through the Depression and hardly slowed down during the Second World War. His

Kenyon Nicholson's successful career as a playwright began in 1921 when he coauthored *Honor Bright* with fellow Crawfordsville native Meredith Nicholson. Kenyon worked on Broadway, in Hollywood and in summer stock at the Bucks County Playhouse in New Jersey, where he retired. *CDPL Photo.*

writing was distinctive in its comedic flair and attention to local color and characters, and he never lost his passion for travel. Kenyon and his wife retired in Stockton, New Jersey, in the 1950s.

Sadly, Kenyon's brilliant mind failed him in his later years. In a letter in the Crawfordsville District Public Library collection, written in 1976 to a friend, Lucile described the fifty-mile round trip to see Kenyon, who was suffering from arteriosclerosis and dementia, in a nursing home: "People tell me I am foolish to make the long trip daily but sometimes he seems to know me and just in case my being there gives him some reassurance, I go." Lucile died two years later; Kenyon died on December 19, 1986, at the age of ninety-two.

From Actress to Author

Maude Snyder

Jodie Steelman Wilson

At first glance, Janet Lambert, the famed local author of fifty-four books for young adults, would not seem to be a candidate for a book on hidden history, since she has received much local attention through the years for her prolific writing career. But writing was not the only talent that won her acclaim beyond Montgomery County; she also appeared on Broadway and acted with William Powell, best known for the *Thin Man* series of movies from the 1930s.

Janet Lambert was named Maude Snyder at her birth in Crawfordsville on December 17, 1893, according to local birth records. Her father was Francis L. Snyder, the first supreme scribe of the Supreme Tribe of Ben-Hur, a founder of the Crawfordsville fraternal insurance organization. He was a civic leader as well as a good businessman and was loyal to Crawfordsville, blocking an attempt by some officials to relocate the Supreme Tribe of Ben-Hur offices to Terre Haute.

As Janet recalled in a letter she wrote to Crawfordsville friend Fern Ream Wallace, her father encouraged the girl's childhood interest in acting, made sure that she could attend local performances of out-of-town performers and took her backstage to meet prominent vaudeville stars such as the extravagant Eva Tanguay, known for her lavish costumes, at Townsley's Music Hall at 122 South Green Street. Although her father actively encouraged her interest in acting, he died in 1906, before he had a chance to see her aspirations realized.

Maude Snyder, the young girl dressed in a fur-trimmed coat, appears in the center of this circa 1895 photograph of the associates of the Supreme Tribe of Ben-Hur. Her father, Frank Snyder, is standing behind Maude, his hand in his pocket. Although the identities of at least some of the other subjects were recorded, the writing on the photograph has faded and can no longer be read. *CDPL Photo.*

In 1911, Maude graduated from Crawfordsville High School, completing her studies in three and a half years. She appeared in the 1909 CHS productions of *The College Widow's Club* and *My Lord in Livery* and in the CHS 1910 Sunshine Society production of *An Open Secret*, as the lead. She later appeared in city dramatic productions, as well.

After high school, her mother sent her to Ferry Hall, a young ladies' finishing school near Chicago. In an interview with the *Beach Haven Times* given late in her life, Janet recalled that she quit the school to study elocution with Mrs. Jennie Ormsby in Indianapolis, and she also remembered the start of her professional dramatic career. She went to see a play performed by the Walker Whiteside Touring Company. She was so eager to act with the group that she found Whiteside backstage and told him that she could play the part of the ingénue much better than the current actress. But no cast changes were made, and the company went on to its next engagement without her.

Then, in November 1915, she received a wire to come at once to New York, where Whiteside had a part for her in a play, *The Typhoon*. She made arrangements, taking along her half sister, Mabel, as a chaperone at her mother's insistence, and

Above, left: Maude Snyder, in her days acting with the Walker Whiteside Touring Company. In March 1916, when the Whiteside traveling company played Crawfordsville's Music Hall, the capacity crowd gave Snyder an ovation that lasted for minutes, and friends and family flooded the stage with baskets of flowers. *Collection of Jeanne Ann Vanderhoef.*

Above, right: William Powell, during his time with the Northampton Players. He and Maude Snyder acted in three productions together in Massachusetts. Powell went on to fame in Hollywood productions, including the *Thin Man* movie series. *Collection of Jeanne Ann Vanderhoef.*

was off for New York. She had previously been cast in a role in the upcoming Wabash College Dramatic Club production of *The Pigeon*, so stage manager Kenyon Nicholson was left scrambling to find a replacement, while members of the Dramatic Club were said to be despairing over their predicament.

In March 1916, the end of the touring season, the production of *The Typhoon* came to Crawfordsville. The *Crawfordsville Review*'s coverage began, "It was 'Maude Snyder Night' at the Music Hall." After the second act, she received a standing ovation from the crowd so heartfelt that the newspaper claimed, "In her future career as an actress, Miss Snyder will not receive such an ovation. She was literally smothered with flowers." A line of ushers presented baskets and bouquets from a group of her friends, store owner

The wedding photograph of Cavalry Officer Kent Lambert and Maude Snyder, January 1, 1918. Maude took advantage of the occasion to change her name from Maude Snyder to Janet Lambert. *Collection of Jeanne Ann Vanderhoef.*

Louis Bischof, the Supreme Tribe of Ben-Hur employees and many others. Whiteside lifted them to the stage himself.

But thrilling though it might have been, it was just the beginning of Maude's acting career. In December 1916, she was offered a Broadway role in the play *Gamblers All*. Although it was a short run with only eight performances, she was then cast in *Nothing but the Truth*, another New York production. Popular leading man William Collier, who has a star on the Hollywood Walk of Fame, was a cast mate. Although the actual timeline is still uncertain, she also acted in three productions of a stock theater company in Northampton, Massachusetts, with fellow actor William Powell, who later found fame in movies. Powell, a friend, presented her with a white Spitz dog she named Tokoramo, after Whiteside's character in her first play, *The Typhoon*. Later she appeared in Boston in the production *Arabian Nights*.

But the end of her acting career was approaching. A mysterious visitor who declined to give his name to the hotel staff dropped by to see her in

New York during a rewrite for the Boston play. Maude opened the door to find Captain Kent Lambert, a Crawfordsville friend who had joined the cavalry. After a whirlwind romance, they married on January 1, 1918, and she took the opportunity to change her first and last names; she would then be known as Janet Lambert. Although Kent had promised that he would not be deployed overseas, just a week after their wedding, he was notified that the cavalry would be sent to Europe. Janet was planning her return to the stage after Kent's departure, at least until an illness sidelined her. After consulting her doctor, she found out that she was expecting a baby and returned to Crawfordsville, where her daughter, Jeanne Ann, was born. With her daughter's birth, Janet's acting career was finished.

When Kent returned from Europe, Janet adjusted to her new role as an army wife and mother, living in many different places around the world as Kent's career advanced. Ultimately, Kent was promoted to colonel and became post commander at Governors Island, New York. Janet began to write in 1936, when her daughter started college and her schedule began to allow free time for writing. After signing a contract with E.P. Dutton, she wrote two books per year for the publishing company until 1972. She enjoyed great popularity with her young readers for her many books and had an active fan club. Janet Lambert died on March 17, 1973, and Kent died on December 17, 1982. They are buried at Oak Hill Cemetery in Crawfordsville.

The Courthouse Tower Is Going to Fall (or Is It?)

Emily Griffin Winfrey

The groundbreaking ceremony for the construction of the new Montgomery County Courthouse was held on August 17, 1874, and its elegant tower was raised into position two years later. With its tower, the courthouse stood a remarkable 155 feet high (about as tall as a fifteen-story building) above the streets of Crawfordsville, and its pleasantly toned bell could be heard for miles around. For sixty-five years, the courthouse tower, with a clock on all four sides (added in November 1876), was a beautiful landmark. The tower, in fact, served a useful purpose for local citizens; the September 9, 1941 *Crawfordsville Journal Review* reported that the clock and its ringing bell "advised visiting farmers that it'd hustle 'em to get home by feedin' time, has been the housewives' time advisor during shopping tours, and has sped the tardy school youngster." But in late 1941, the tower was demolished after an order by the county commissioners.

When the new courthouse with its tower and clock intact was dedicated, there was a great deal of fanfare, and local newspapers provided detailed descriptions of the construction process. But when the clock and its bell were silenced in 1941, so was any detailed reason explaining why the tower had come down. The only article that describes the tower's fate does not provide a date for the removal or reasoning for the decision other than to say that the tower had been condemned. It remains a mystery that the unexplained condemnation and destruction of such a beloved landmark produced so little community conversation at the time.

The impressive courthouse tower, decorated for the Grand Army of the Republic state encampment in 1909. The courthouse, with its four-faced clock made to order from Boston, was first dedicated in 1876. The courthouse, with its tower intact, stood high above the rest of the town. *CDPL Photo.*

Although few details are given, the 1941 article does note that the removal would cost $3,900. According to the November 25, 1876 *Crawfordsville Weekly Review*, the tower clock originally accounted for $1,239.30 of the $130,000.00 total spent to build the new courthouse. When the courthouse tower clock arrived from Boston, where it had been made to order, it was exhibited in Mat Klein's store at 31 East Main Street. The *Crawfordsville Review*, on November 4, remarked on "the beauty of the works and the elegance of their finish" and noted that "every wheel and cog is finished with wonderful delicacy and exactness."

No one seemed to object to this delicate piece coming down, but townspeople did have other matters on their minds. World War II was approaching, and Montgomery County residents were committed to the war effort. In 2011, Rebecca Neideffer, author of a Montgomery County Courthouse history, stated that the Depression and war were all she could find to explain the lack of interest: "I can only guess that everyone was so concerned about their personal welfare and the future of the country to give much thought to funds being spent for the courthouse."

This painting (circa 1930s) by artist Fritz Schlemmer was perhaps the reason the tower was taken down. In 1941, the tower was removed after this painting, in which the tower appears to be leaning, sparked concerns. *Chase Bank.*

One person preoccupied with the war was Dr. Marion Kirtley. As he related in his autobiography, *Kirtley Kronicles*, "I had been aware of that stately old clock all my life and the deep 'bong' of the bell could be heard all over town. When the wind was from the north and east, the sounds were sweet and clear and gave one the feeling that all was right in Crawfordsville. The

Lee Detchon, a student of artist Fritz Schlemmer, completed this watercolor painting that shows a view of the courthouse with its tower from North Washington Street. The tower appears to be leaning in this painting, but it is unknown whether the painting was based on a photograph, another painting or the courthouse as it actually stood. *CDPL Photo.*

last time I heard the clock strike was in December 1940, as I was preparing to report to the United States Army for active duty as a medical reservist." When Kirtley arrived home on leave in 1941, he was shocked to find that the meaningful emblem overlooking his hometown had disappeared. Kirtley expressed his discontent at the new sight, "a truncated tower that had removed the dignity from a stately building. What defacement, I thought!"

The tower's condition had been considered an issue as early as the 1930s, when respected local artist Fritz Schlemmer did a painting of the courthouse for Bud and June Zeller. In the painting, the tower does appear to be leaning significantly. Former researchers have credited this painting with the later destruction of the courthouse tower. Because Schlemmer saw and painted the tower in a leaning condition, commissioners felt that the tower was a hazard. An advocate for the tower's restoration, Kirtley was unable to find details in the commissioners' records but often heard that the story of Schlemmer's painting held "considerable weight" in the decision. With patriotism in mind, Montgomery County commissioners were able to support the war effort by donating the 1,061-pound bell to the metal collecting effort. Obviously, it seemed more important to contribute to the war effort than to save the tower at the time.

The bell became a symbol of the county's dedication to the war effort, but the actual clock would be stripped of its dignity as it was stored outside in the elements at the highway department garage for the next twenty-six years, according to the *Journal Review* of May 19, 1971. Leonard Winchell and Hubert Danzebrink purchased the clock after attempts to place it in the Boulevard Mall proved impractical. Crawfordsville is lucky that Danzebrink and Winchell had a personal interest in the clock. If they had not cared so deeply about its repair, the clock would have been sold to a scrap dealer. Danzebrink restored the clock in the early 1970s, which was not an easy feat because the clock was in 130 parts, with 125 bolts and screws. Initially, Danzebrink could not tell which parts were brass and which were steel because they were so heavily coated in oil. Interestingly, the same oil build-up prevented serious damage to the clock in the twenty years that it stood outside in the rain. Depending on their disrepair, pieces had to be glass-blasted and chrome-plated. The only new piece added to the clock was a cable; all other parts are original. The historical clock's mechanism, now more than 130 years old, is in Winchell's downtown building, directly across the street from the courthouse.

But did the commissioners make the right decision? Was the tower actually in danger of collapsing, or did a local painting create a great deal of panic over nothing? Resident Sandy Lofland-Brown doubts that the tower was ever dangerous. Commissioners were worried that the tower (made of heavy wood and iron) was ready to fall, but it didn't seem to fall easily in 1941. Lofland-Brown stated, "It took three months to get it down because it was so secure and steady." Danzebrink agreed that the tower was "supposed to be leaning, but I heard they had a hard time getting it down. I can't imagine they would put a flimsy tower on such a foundation." Recently, the courthouse tower committee hired a structural engineer to evaluate the safety of a tower. The engineer found that the support area for the original tower is still intact and sturdy enough to support a new tower.

George Bunting, Indianapolis architect, designed the Montgomery County Courthouse in addition to seven other courthouses in Indiana. Two of the original courthouses have been replaced with modern structures. Of the six remaining, only the Montgomery County Courthouse is without a tower. However, there had been a tower issue at the Union County Courthouse in Liberty, Indiana, in 1891. Right after construction finished in July 1891, the

Union County Courthouse tower collapsed, but it was rebuilt within nine months, according to *Magnificent 92: Indiana Courthouses*. The courthouse and its tower are safely standing today. It is unclear whether commissioners knew of this previous tower failure as they examined Schlemmer's painting and made their decision.

Commissioners had discussed removing the tower years before the painting, but not because of a leaning condition. In 1913, Montgomery County commissioners reasoned that if fire were to reach the tower, saving the courthouse would be impossible. Not wanting to risk important legal records and seeking a more fireproof structure, commissioners agreed that

The Montgomery County Courthouse, located at 100 East Main Street, as it looks today without its elegant tower. In recent years, a committee has worked to restore a tower back to the courthouse. The original clock, restored by Hubert Danzebrink, is located in the Winchell building in downtown Crawfordsville. *CDPL Photo.*

the tower should be removed. They planned to make use of this top area, though. On December 30, the *Crawfordsville Daily Journal* revealed future plans to add a third story to the courthouse. The third story, with a new fireproof roof, would be used as a courtroom so that the second floor could be composed of rooms for county officers. The tower, of course, would not come down for another twenty-eight years.

Despite the efforts of a recent committee, the courthouse is still without a tower. In 1996, Sandy Lofland-Brown, Luther Lofland and Dr. Marion Kirtley created a courthouse tower committee and began to raise money to restore the courthouse to its former glory. Kirtley, still devastated by the loss of the tower while at war, considered the tower's renovation to be his personal mission. Although Kirtley had accomplished so much in his lifetime, the restoration of the tower was, according to Sandy Lofland-Brown, "the only thing he felt he'd been unable to accomplish in his life." The retired doctor's autobiography was printed and donated by R.R. Donnelley & Sons so that proceeds could benefit his project. In his autobiography, Kirtley expressed hope that the tower bell would ring again in his lifetime. Kirtley's wish would not come true. He died in 2000, but before he passed, he made Sandy Lofland-Brown promise to continue the restoration project without him.

With the economic downturn of the new century, it's been hard to move forward with the project. The committee is actively pursuing funding but does not qualify for many available grants because the courthouse structure is not endangered. Lofland-Brown described the tough situation at hand: "The project is still on. I always say it's not *if*, it's *when* it happens. It's just hard to ask people in the community to give money for a beautification project when the economy is bad. Of course, it would be much more than that. It's not just a tower. It's a significant part of our history." The clock, too, has been forgotten over the years. In the past, thousands would visit Winchell's building to see the clock, but now people rarely stop by to see its workings. Hubert Danzebrink would love to see a new tower placed on the courthouse. As he put it, "You've got to have something for your eyes to enjoy. When you go to England, you want to see the palace." Townspeople have grown accustomed to a flat-topped courthouse, but when visitors come to downtown Crawfordsville, they see a chopped-off, unfinished building. Let's return the crown to our courthouse and give them a palace on which to feast their eyes.

Crawfordsville's Thomas Edison

Shirl Herr

Jodie Steelman Wilson

What do Italian Fascist ruler Benito Mussolini and Admiral Richard Byrd, Antarctic explorer, have in common? Crawfordsville resident Shirl Herr helped both in tackling otherwise impossible-to-solve problems with his invention, the magnetic balance, a very early prototype of the metal detector. Although he is perhaps better known locally for his civic leadership and position as cofounder of Crawfordsville Seed Company, Herr's inventions and collaboration with scientists took him on adventures the world over, including a 1929 treasure hunting excursion with Mussolini himself.

Shirl Herr was born in Lapland, in southern Montgomery County, in 1875. As a young man, he and his family moved to Boone County. In an article published in the *Crawfordsville Journal Review*, his son, Remley Herr, noted that the majority of his education took place in a one-room schoolhouse. Family members indicated that his education ended at the eighth grade.

Despite his lack of higher education, he could envision possibilities that others could not, as his brother, John, recounted in his book, *Shirl, My Brother*. As a young man, Shirl conceived the idea of air soles for athletic shoes. He had carried on experiments inserting pneumatic tubes into the sole of shoes to give athletes an advantage in competition. Although athletes of the time encouraged him to continue with his experiments, he never filed a patent on his idea, and his lack of finances caused it to be abandoned.

Portrait of Shirl Herr, who is wearing the headset that allowed him to hear the buzz indicating a nearby metal item. He is holding the battery box under his left arm and the magnetic balance in his right hand. Photograph by Nellie Coutant. *Collection of the Herr family.*

Shirl's conception of a coated powder critical to preventing premature explosions in the firing of high-explosive shells, as well as the resulting experiments, received publicity in the *New York Tribune* and in other sources around the world, according to his brother John's account. Previous technology used compressed air to safely launch high explosives. The Washington, D.C. Ordnance Department wrote to Shirl that his theory was absolutely correct, and local U.S. Representative Charles Landis visited the department on Shirl's behalf, where he was again congratulated on the development. Another of his ideas was called "cold light," which was, in essence, the theory behind compact fluorescent light technology.

In 1906, he was granted his first patent, for a color-changing device that could be used to project a beam of light that changed slowly from one color to another color and rotated through all colors of the rainbow. In the era of the nickelodeon, Shirl saw a potential for profit, but with his limited resources, he didn't have the capital necessary to invest in the concept. Shortly after the first patent, he patented a process to remove weed seeds from clover seeds. John Herr, Shirl's brother, pitched the idea to the Crabbs Reynolds Taylor Seed Company in Crawfordsville, and it interested the partners greatly. But because the output of the machine Shirl had designed was too small, they told John to come back when Shirl had a machine that could process twenty-five bushels per day. Very shortly, Shirl had increased the output to their specifications and was hired to go to Chicago, New York and Toronto to build similar machines there.

As a foreman at the Crabbs Reynolds Taylor Seed Company, Shirl didn't have a particularly lucrative or impressive job. His family did not possess a great fortune or have well-connected family members. In 1910, when he married Sallie Remley, the daughter of wealthy Crawfordsville Civil War veteran Ambrose Remley, one local store responded to the news by cancelling her credit account. Despite this evident lack of faith in Shirl's future success, there is an ironic twist to the story: the money later earned by his inventions made it possible, according to family sources, for his fortune to support the Elston Bank through the Great Depression. This support was a closely guarded secret, since Shirl realized that the bank would fail if depositors suspected that it was financially unstable. Although the story cannot now be independently verified, it is certainly true that Shirl's career as an inventor was financially rewarding.

As a result of the success of the clover seed-separating machine and later refinements, Shirl was able to found Crawfordsville Seed Company with A.H. Flanigan in 1914. The financial security established by his seed company made it possible for him to travel and spend time on his inventions. Shirl's experiments had one goal, according to John Herr: the discovery of new knowledge. Any financial considerations were secondary concerns, and having his theories later proven correct was his ultimate reward. He would take up new theories, investigate them until all his questions had been answered to his satisfaction and then move on to a new project without regard to financial gain.

Until 1924, most of Shirl's projects had been theoretical, and they were not completed into finished products except for his seed-cleaning inventions. But in 1924, he applied for a patent on a hidden-metal detector, an invention that would prove to be his most famous. This patent was not granted until 1928. A second patent, for an underground prospecting device, was granted about the same time.

In August 1929, while the Herr family vacationed in Rome, Shirl Herr offered the use of his "magnetic balance" to assist the Italian government in discovering artifacts obscured in the deep mud at the bottom of Lake Nemi. The Emperor Caligula had used the lake for a summer resort, and when his luxurious galleys kept there were sunk, the figureheads, furnishings and fittings, some of solid gold, settled into the tarlike lake floor. At the time of Herr's trip, Lake Nemi was being drained in an Italian government program intended to recover Roman antiquities, with the hope of boosting tourism. The water had receded enough to uncover the first of the two boats by the time of Shirl Herr's arrival.

Son Remley Herr went along on this excursion, and he remembered it in an article written in the *Crawfordsville Journal Review* published July 23, 1975. He wrote that a chauffeur-driven black limousine arrived at their hotel in Rome to pick them up, and Mussolini himself was waiting inside. As they made their way to Lake Nemi, Mussolini, trying to overcome the language barrier, indicated that the road was the same that Caligula himself would have used for the journey.

Upon their arrival at the site, Remley recalled that the boats looked "no more romantic than a big pile of heavily-creosoted railroad ties dumped like jackstraws on the mud floor of an out-sized gravel pit." Planking laid next to the boats allowed Shirl, carrying the magnetic balance, and Remley, carrying the battery box, to move around freely. Repeatedly, Shirl would call "Here!" and a workman would jump into the mud to retrieve metal pieces. Some were lead fountain pieces, others made of iron. Occasionally, a solid gold figurehead would be retrieved from the black ooze.

Wearied after a long day of hunting, Shirl was drawn out to the edge of the planking by a strong buzz. Hoping to pinpoint the source, he twisted over to the side…and fell right into the mud. Although Shirl was unharmed, his magnetic balance wouldn't work again until overhauled. Worse, in trying to clean up after the accident, Shirl realized that he was covered with large, black leeches. Remley recorded that the discovery greatly expedited the removal of both mud and clothes.

Although the day ended prematurely, Shirl's contribution to the effort allowed far more artifacts to be recovered than would have been found and documented otherwise. Unfortunately, as the Nazis fled the area around Lake Nemi during World War II, they set fire to the restored galleys, at that time housed in a museum at Lake Nemi.

On other trips, Shirl investigated meteorites in Arizona with Dr. Charles Clayton Wiley, professor at the University of Iowa, and searched for artifacts at Hadrian's Wall in northern England with Remley. With Dr. Raymond Abbott of Purdue University, Shirl was invited to use the magnetic balance to search in Uniontown, Pennsylvania, for artifacts from Braddock's Defeat, a 1755 British military expedition attempted during the French and Indian War. The search uncovered many relics and, according to John Herr, caused scholars to realize that the route once

Remley Herr and Shirl Herr (wearing the headset for his magnetic balance) take a break on an excursion. Remley is holding items recovered with the early magnetic detector's assistance. *Collection of the Herr family.*

believed to have been General Braddock's retreat was not correct, as the placement of the artifacts indicated.

Thomas Poulter, physics professor at Iowa Wesleyan College, met Shirl Herr in Arizona in 1932. After being named second-in-command to Admiral Richard E. Byrd on Byrd's second Antarctic expedition, Poulter visited Crawfordsville and announced that he would be taking Shirl Herr's magnetic balance, altered to be both snow-proof and waterproof, along on the trip. The machine proved to be very useful on the expedition by locating the site of Little America, Byrd's base camp from his previous expedition several years before, a great help because of the still-usable provisions buried there by ice and snow. Poulter reported that the balance was effective, even at the depth of eight feet.

Shirl missed few opportunities to travel across the country in the interest of scientific discovery. And on one occasion, he was able to help his academic friends at home in Crawfordsville by helping to expose what C.C. Wylie called "the Crawfordsville Meteorite Hoax." On October 10, 1930, seventeen-year-old Lawrence Swank of Crawfordsville reported that his car had been struck by an object that tore through the hood and radiator as he was driving south of town on the Terre Haute Road, presently State Route 47. He said, noted the *Journal Review* published October 11, 1930, that he believed it was "holdup men" but that he didn't see any lights in the rural area where he was driving. After returning to the scene in daylight, Swank and his father located a hole in the road surface about half an inch deep. No trace of the meteor was found at the site, but a small piece of carborundum, common in space, was found under the generator.

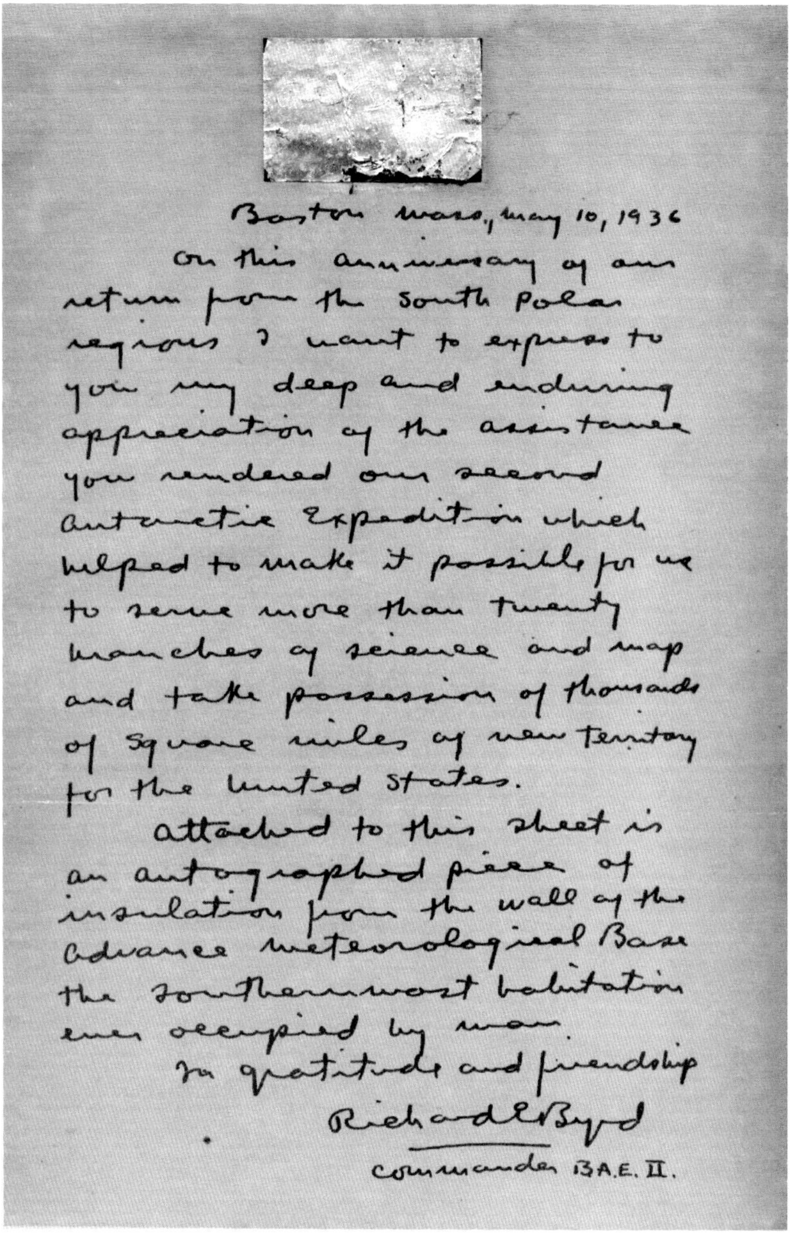

Boston Mass., May 10, 1936

On this anniversary of our return from the South Polar regions I want to express to you my deep and enduring appreciation of the assistance you rendered our second Antarctic Expedition which helped to make it possible for us to serve more than twenty branches of science and map and take possession of thousands of square miles of new territory for the United States.

Attached to this sheet is an autographed piece of insulation from the wall of the Advance Meteorological Base the southernmost habitation ever occupied by man.

In gratitude and friendship

Richard E Byrd

Commander B.A.E. II.

The letter from Admiral Richard Byrd to Shirl Herr concerning the Second Byrd Antarctic Mission to the South Pole (1933–35). In the letter, Admiral Byrd thanks Herr and expresses his appreciation for Herr's assistance in sending a magnetic balance to Antarctica with the expeditioners. This assistance made it possible for Byrd's team to serve more than twenty branches of science and map and take possession of thousands of square miles of new territory for the United States. *Collection of the Herr family.*

The press had a field day with the news. Lawrence Swank's story and the photograph of Swank posing by the damaged Ford were run in media outlets across the United States and abroad over a span of months. C.C. Wylie, in an article in *Popular Astronomy* published in 1948, wrote that the story appeared in periodicals such as *The Literary Digest*, *Popular Science Monthly*, *Pathfinder* and *Science and Invention*. Dozens of newspapers such as the *Palm Beach Post*, *Milwaukee Sentinel* and *Boston Globe* carried the story. But Wylie had suspicions that the whole truth had not been revealed, and he enlisted Shirl's help in studying the event, finding the evidence and asking questions of the participants.

Shirl and Professor G.E. Carscallen of Wabash College investigated the story to verify its facts. They believed that Swank was telling the truth, as far as he knew. However, they did determine that Swank had not mentioned a whizzing noise the first time he told his story. After the meteor idea had been introduced, he thought he remembered a noise. Swank did not see a streak of fire as the "meteorite" hit, and no local person had seen a meteor that could be associated with the damage done to Swank's car. Meteors stop glowing at about fifteen miles of altitude and fall to the earth invisibly at night. The scratches in the hole in the pavement were inconsistent with the direction of the projectile. Finally, the idea of the meteor was suggested not by Lawrence Swank but by a worker at the garage where his car was taken for repair.

Many scientific reasons were found why the damage could not have been from a meteorite. A meteor large enough to survive the descent to the earth's surface to hit the car would have been large enough to have been seen by residents of adjoining states. Although a meteor was reportedly seen in Crawfordsville, it was not possible to make any association between the sighted meteor and the location of the car. The angle of the hole was inconsistent with a meteor. Meteors large enough to fall to the earth are nearly always accompanied with an explosion louder than thunder, followed by a roar. The sound is very different from a simple gunshot, and this is what Lawrence Swank had reported. C.C. Wylie summarized the episode in an article, "Did a Meteorite Strike the Crawfordsville Ford?" published in *Scientific American* in March 1931. A map, drawn to accompany the article, was created by Shirl Herr.

Wylie's explanation of the story was that it was a clever practical joke being played on Swank. Although a bit of carborundum had been found embedded in the generator, it was man-made. In April 1931, the *Journal Review* reported that Wylie attributed the holes in the roadster's hood and radiator to a shotgun and no. 4 shot at close range. Although the local newspaper account of the confessions has not been found (if there was one), in the *Popular Astronomy* article in 1948, C.C. Wylie pronounced the incident "the most successful scientific hoax of the last 50 years" and said that the perpetrators of the hoax eventually came forward after the investigation had been completed.

All in all, Shirl Herr's contributions to scientific knowledge were impressive for any man, without regard to level of education. But education itself is not the most important quality needed for scientific achievement. Shirl himself said that "higher learning would not have been good for me…I've been told, too often, by physicists and engineers, that certain things couldn't be done and could be proved impossible by the books. Only I found that those things sometimes could be done." An open mind, a creative mind, able to grasp the questions and find the answers is obviously more important than education as a qualification for solving problems. Montgomery County, and the world at large, has been enriched by this local man and his uncanny ability to see solutions where others could not.

Disgraced Doctors

Rebecca McDole

Frauds, fakes, hermits and thieves…the medicine men of Montgomery County have pasts that are littered with sordid tales and shocking crimes. Whether it was stealing from Uncle Sam or from unsuspecting dupes, killing patients or themselves, doctors were making headlines from the time the county was formed. These stories, now forgotten, were once the talk of the town.

Dr. Israel T. Canby

Following the Revolutionary War, as people began drifting west into unknown territories, the United States government established the Land Office to oversee the surveying and sale of public lands. After numerous revisions, Congress passed a law in 1820 offering eighty-acre tracts of land at $1.25 per acre. When the Land Office relocated to Crawfordsville from Terre Haute in 1823, city founder Ambrose Whitlock was appointed receiver of public monies—until he was abruptly ousted from office to make way for Dr. Israel T. Canby.

Canby, father of Civil War general E.R.S. Canby, came to Indiana in 1818. Although he studied medicine at an eastern medical college, it is unclear whether he actually earned a degree, and his activities in politics seem to have left him little time to practice. He served in the state legislature from 1821 to 1822 and again as a senator from 1826 to 1828. After an unsuccessful campaign for governor in 1828, Canby turned to his influential Jacksonian friends in Washington; with their help, for "services rendered to the party in the past," Canby was awarded Ambrose Whitlock's job as receiver of public monies. Whitlock was furious. After being forced to surrender the keys to his office, Mr. Whitlock "commenced…warfare upon the Doctor" and heaped abuse on the doctor's character and ethics, according to the *Crawfordsville Record* on August 10, 1832. Whitlock's vindication was not long in coming. In 1833, scandal hit the Land Office.

"In consequence of a misapplication of some forty or fifty thousand of Uncle Sam's cash," Canby was removed from office, and an investigation into his activities was initiated. It was found that Canby had financed a mercantile operation and extended loans to friends with money from the Land Office. It was not an uncommon practice among receivers like Canby to use public funds for their private purposes; at the time of Canby's disgrace, five other officers also owed Uncle Sam, but Canby's debt was by far the largest. The doctor skipped town for a while to secure the support of friends like Senators Tipton and Hendricks and returned home with every appearance of earnestly wanting to make good on his debt.

But Canby may not have been as sincerely repentant as he appeared: he deeded goods to partners so they could not be seized, he directed the sales of his lands so that the best lots were saved for himself and he proclaimed at the sale of his estate that "no gentleman would bid on the property," according to the *Crawfordsville Record* of January 3, 1835. Most of the goods from the estate sale were purchased at the minimum price by his sister and housekeeper. Claims dragged on until 1870, when Congress absolved his descendants of liability. But at the time of his death in 1846, Dr. Canby's estate was in the black—he was worth about $20,000, the equivalent of about $500,000 today.

DR. G.W. EDDINGFIELD

In 1899, Dr. George Williamson Eddingfield learned the truth of the saying "Any advertising is good advertising" when a patient brought an unusual lawsuit against the doctor.

Dr. Eddingfield, a longtime resident of Montgomery County, received his medical degree from Miami University at Cincinnati in 1872 and hung his shingle in Mace shortly after. In the small room he used for an office on his property, the doctor charged patients $0.25, $0.50 or $1.00 for his services; for a house call, the patient paid $2.00. According to his record book from 1894 to 1903, Eddingfield didn't give family discounts—he charged his mother and brothers the same as anyone else. After more than twenty-five years serving the Mace community, Dr. Eddingfield had earned its warm friendship and respect, and shock was felt all around when Thomas Burk sued Eddingfield for $5,000.00 (more than $100,000.00 today).

Burk, a laborer, alleged that on July 12, 1899, Dr. Eddingfield was called to attend Burk's wife as she gave birth, but he refused to come. Burk said he called again and even sent Reverend Riley on his behalf with the doctor's fee, and still Eddingfield did not come. As a result of the doctor's refusal, Burk claimed, his wife and child died.

In his defense, Dr. Eddingfield gave compelling reasons for refusing Burk's pleas. First, he was already attending a patient whose case was just as dire as Mrs. Burk's. Second, there were other physicians nearby who could have taken the case—in fact, another doctor did but was unable to save the mother or child. Lastly, Dr. Eddingfield refuted the claim that Reverend Riley begged for his help or offered him money.

The case *Burk v. Eddingfield* was a sensation in Montgomery County, as it was the first of its kind, and it is still cited in law schools to this day. Every businessman and professional watched with interest for the verdict: if a

Dr. George Williamson Eddingfield was born in Butler County, Ohio, in 1844 and came with his parents to Crawfordsville in 1858. Dr. Eddingfield practiced in Montgomery County for more than twenty-five years. Eddingfield noted in his record book in May 1897, November 1897 and March 1898 that he had quit tobacco. The room he used for his office was supposedly bought by the Knights of Pythias and used as a barbershop. *CDPL Photo.*

doctor could be called to account for not attending a patient, the October 30, 1899 *Crawfordsville Sunday Star* wondered, "who knows but what it may be held good law that a man is entitled to judgement for damages against a newspaper that fails to print all the news" or a grocer for failing to deliver groceries on time or a preacher for not having a new sermon every Sunday. In the trial, with the firm of Clodfelter and Fine representing him, Eddingfield prevailed.

The *Crawfordsville New Review* on October 28, 1899, had this to say after the trial: "Dr. Eddingfield has suddenly awakened to the fact that he is advertised as never before as a skilled and distinguished physician whose failure to respond when called upon is worth $5,000 to the person refused." The bereaved Mr. Burk, who never remarried, died of progressive anemia in 1909. Dr. Eddingfield continued to practice medicine and died in a Cleveland hospital on December 1, 1926.

DR. WILLIAM DECAUX TILNEY

The life of William DeCaux Tilney reads like a classic novel. Born in Norwich, England, in 1841, Tilney quit school at twelve to work ten-hour days in a shoe factory, hoarding his money to buy books. In 1859, he joined the medical staff of the British army fighting in India, where he served for four years until he was disabled by sunstroke. After studying at Oxford and trying his hand at medicine back in England—where, he told the *Crawfordsville Saturday Evening Journal* in 1877, he was "ostracized and came near to starving"—Tilney came to America and settled in Chicago. He took odd jobs wherever he could find them and tried to "live on less eating, the hardest work for an Englishman." Giving up on the life of a workingman, Tilney "engaged a man to talk" and took to the road to peddle his medicines. He came to Crawfordsville in 1865, making this city his base of operations.

Traveling to Colorado in March 1900, the doctor, advertising himself as a "Miracle Worker," had rented the Park Opera House in Grand Junction to deliver free lectures. Things were going well for the doctor and his cohorts; to the amazement of their audience, they made the deaf hear and the crippled walk after just twenty minutes with his medicines. But when rumors of a scandal destroyed his business, Tilney packed his bags and hightailed it to the train station, where he was apprehended by Sheriff Charles Wallis and charged with the murder of Edward Skinner.

In 1877, Dr. William DeCaux Tilney delivered a series of free lectures in Waveland on the subjects of love, courtship and marriage. The doctor believed in "speaking plainly and calling things by their right names," much to the consternation of his young audience, many of whom blushingly took the first opportunity to "slide out from under his elocutionary range," according to the *Crawfordsville Star* of May 10, 1877. Tilney and his wife, in the same lectures, refuted spiritualism by using steel rods bandaged inside their sleeves to transport a heavy table. *CDPL Photo.*

Skinner's widow testified that her husband had come to Grand Junction on Thursday to see Dr. Tilney's miracles in person and was so impressed that he paid fifty dollars to take some home, where he then sent for more of the medicine. But by Sunday, Mr. Skinner was dead. The general opinion was that the miracle cure Tilney sold contained large quantities of aconite and other drugs. Tilney countered that his medicine was no different than that prescribed by any other doctor and that his arrest was the result of the flock of jealous physicians he had offended by invading their territory.

Tilney got the last word; the *Crawfordsville Daily Journal* reported on April 5, 1900, that District Attorney Samuel G. McMullen dropped the murder charge after a chemical analysis of the medicine showed that it "would not kill a mouse." The slandered Tilney vowed to bring damage suits against the people of Grand Junction and the newspapers that had libeled him so unjustly.

In his *Daily Journal* obituary of October 12, 1925, Dr. William DeCaux Tilney was remembered as a learned man and a very interesting character who continuously educated himself in the medical profession.

"DOC" WILLIS

The tallest grave marker in Alamo Cemetery belongs to Joseph Martin "Doc" Willis of Alamo. Willis was not technically a doctor. He had no medical training or expertise, but that did not deter him from developing and selling his patented medicine, the famous Pansy Compound. A purely vegetable-based remedy, the compound also contained roots, herbs, barks and gums and was purported to be a permanent cure for all chronic diseases. "Doc" Willis, according to the *Daily Journal* on November 13, 1903, was a "man of many unusual traits" and worked in the Lew Fisher Drug Store on North Green Street in Crawfordsville before returning home in 1902 to Alamo, where he built himself a home and business.

Described as a "recluse" by the *Daily Journal*, Willis was a taciturn man, seldom speaking to anyone. His disappearance the first week of November 1903 had gone unnoticed, but when someone casually remarked, "Where is 'Doc' Willis?" a party was organized to investigate. His body was soon discovered with a "ragged hole in the center of his forehead," an apparent suicide. The *Daily Journal* article of November 13 called him a "victim of melancholia."

The tragic suicide took a strange turn when a note was found pinned to the bed in front of Willis's corpse. The note was written on a sheet of foolscap paper measuring thirty-six inches in length (although the *Daily Journal* reported that it was five feet long). The *Daily Journal* printed the note in full three days after his death, on November 14, 1903. Willis wrote that his suicide was "in contemplation for some time." He was sensitive, his family had turned against him and he would "bid adieu to this mundane

The impressive monument to Joseph Martin "Doc" Willis looms over the other grave markers at Alamo Cemetery. *CDPL Photo.*

sphere." He included very specific instructions. First, Willis asked to be cremated, at a cost of thirty-five dollars. Funeral director D.C. Barnhill was required to accompany the body to St. Louis for the cremation. Next, he wanted the money from his estate, after his debts were paid, to go toward paying a band to play at his funeral, with the remainder to be used to build a monument to him.

Not just any band would do, though. Willis wanted a first-class band, the *Daily Journal* reported on November 14, with the Crawfordsville band to play only as a last resort ("their music is not entertaining"). He suggested the Marine or Military Band of Indianapolis or the Ringgold Band of Terre Haute. The funeral, however, was conducted without a band at all, with everyone blaming someone else for failing to follow "Doc's" instructions.

The last wish of "Doc" Willis, the raising of a monument in his honor, was fulfilled. At a cost of $2,600, the sixty-ton granite monument was shipped from New York to Waynetown, where it was pulled by horse-drawn carriages to Alamo. It towers over the other markers and is nine feet three inches square at the base. It stands as a reminder of the lonely life and strange death of Joseph Martin Willis.

Strangely, for each of these men, the crimes and mishaps in their personal or professional lives didn't color the county's opinion of them. Drs. Eddingfield and Tilney continued to practice medicine, Dr. Canby had the respect of the papers when he died and, despite his strange quirks, "Doc" Willis inspired sympathy in his community. It would seem Montgomery County had a soft spot for scoundrels.

Carrie Nation Cleans Up Crawfordsville

Emily Griffin Winfrey

In the early 1900s, extending an invitation to Carrie Nation could lead to the complete physical destruction of a city's storefronts. The Crawfordsville Elks took this risk when they asked Carrie Nation to attend the city's annual Fourth of July celebration in 1901. Notorious for wielding a hatchet to tear down the saloons and gambling establishments she despised, Nation took pride in her national nickname of the Kansas Smasher. It is surprising, though, that the face of the temperance movement could still elicit fear and excitement as a stout fifty-four-year-old woman.

During the summer of 1901, the citizens of Crawfordsville certainly anticipated Nation's visit with a combination of excitement and fear. A week before her arrival, the Elks gave notice that, as a lodge, they would not take responsibility for any damage that Carrie might cause while in town. The Elks assured that they would arrange for Carrie to avoid her usual destruction and stick to a lecture. However, saloonkeepers were not so certain of this arrangement, and in preparation, they ordered lumber and covered their storefronts. On June 24, the *Crawfordsville Sunday Star* reported that saloonkeeper Charles "Skid" Galey received from Carrie Nation notice that she intended to make a personal inspection of his saloon at 129 North Washington Street.

Townspeople feared Nation's wrath but were excited that such a sensational figure had chosen to visit their city. Concerned after seeing advertisements that placed Nation in other cities for that particular day, the Elks sent a message to remind Nation of her contract. J.J. Insley received a telegram in return. Carrie Nation had not forgotten her promise and would arrive in Crawfordsville on the evening of July 3. Speculation about Nation's arrival continued throughout the first week in July. The July 1, 1901 *Crawfordsville Star* reported that a large amount of mail addressed to Carrie Nation was at the post office that showed that she "is not far away at this time. She may be expected to drop in at any moment." Two days later, on Wednesday, July 3, at 6:15 p.m., Nation arrived. She traveled from a speaking engagement in St. Louis, Missouri, on the Vandalia line. J.J. Insley, Mace Townsley, C.E. Gilbert and Mayor Elmore formed the committee that greeted Nation, clothed in a black bonnet and linen duster style over-dress, at the train station. The *Star* on July 8 noted that J.J. Insley later proudly remarked, "I said I'd get Carrie for them. Well, I did."

A smiling Carrie acknowledged the crowd that had gathered in front of the Crawford Hotel as she checked into her room. According to the July 5 edition of the *Crawfordsville Weekly Journal*, she registered as "Carrie Nation, your only defender, Kansas" in the hotel's guestbook. Locals had a laugh

Carrie Nation stayed in room 200 ("one of the choicest in the hostelry") of the Crawford Hotel on July 3, 1901, the night before her parade and speech. Nation attempted to break into the hotel bar to make a scene in the early hours of July 4 but was not successful. The Crawford Hotel was located at the intersection of Main and Green Streets. *CDPL Photo.*

as they watched Nation gulp two glasses of punch that they had flavored with rum, Nation's enemy. Once she had eaten an informal supper, Nation entertained callers with stories of her crusade: "When I go hunting, I go after game and always bring something down. Crawfordsville is my game this time. What are these Elks, anyhow, that's what I want to know. Why do they name their society after an animal? I guess it is because it has the biggest horns. Isn't that it? Oh, you can't fool me. I want to know all about them and their horns." She declared her intention to save Crawfordsville's "poor lost Elks" before expressing an interest to walk downtown with her hatchet. J.J. Insley and M.E. Foley managed to divert Nation by offering to answer tough questions about their religious and recreational inclinations. Afraid that being out in town on Wednesday might lower the attendance for her big speech on Thursday morning, Nation was satisfied to intimidate the Elks in her hotel room.

On the morning of July 4, Nation, in a suit of white duck, attempted to break into the locked hotel bar to make a scene before harassing a cigarette-smoking night clerk instead. She verbally attacked several men who were smoking tobacco on the sidewalk before taking her place in the parade. Following the parade, Nation was the main attraction. Atop the grandstand with many local dignitaries and introduced by Mayor Elmore, Nation proclaimed the dangers of alcohol, tobacco and saloons while quoting text from the Bible. As she was finishing her speech, Nation's exuberant crowd rushed from the amphitheater onto the stage. The four-foot-tall grandstand crashed under the weight, causing Nation and a dozen of her fans to fall along with it.

Bruised but in good spirits, Nation sold souvenir pictures, pamphlets and miniature hatchets at the fairgrounds. Nation was so successful with her sales that the *Crawfordsville Daily News Review* remarked, "It is the general opinion of those who heard and talked with Mrs. Nation that she is out for the coin of the realm and she will get it too." The July 5, 1901 *Weekly Journal* also questioned Nation's sincerity: "Carrie's fad is her business and she works it for all it is worth. If the doubts could be removed that she really is in earnest in her crusade, she would be reckoned as one of the smoothest grafters that ever struck this town."

Nation was not the only one who benefited from the event, however. The Elks made $300.00 from their efforts. Montgomery County adults paid only $0.25 for admission, while children were charged $0.15 for a full day that included horse races, dancers, acrobats, jugglers, a baseball game, fireworks and the wedding of locals Earl Schular and Berta Ellis. An estimated crowd

Carrie Nation left Crawfordsville on July 5 after touring the city and speaking on the dangers of alcohol and tobacco. Before departing Crawfordsville, Nation posed for this portrait at Nicholson and Sons studio. Note the miniature hatchet pinned to her blouse. *CDPL Photo.*

of seven thousand flocked to witness what the July 3, 1901 *Crawfordsville Daily Journal* deemed "the most pretentious celebration of the glorious day that Crawfordsville has ever witnessed."

It is clear that Carrie Nation enjoyed her visit to Crawfordsville. She even managed to do a minor bit of destruction: persuading young boys to smash beer and wine bottles in a ring at the fairgrounds. Before departing for her home in Topeka, Kansas, on Friday morning, Nation visited Wabash College and the Lew Wallace home. She attended the Passion Play, a presentation of scenes set to music that depicted Christ's crucifixion, at Louis Bischof's Big Store, and posed for a portrait at the local Nicholson and Sons studio situated at 118 East Main Street.

This portrait, preserved in Crawfordsville District Public Library's archives, shows a stern but alert Carrie sitting in a white blouse with a dark scarf. Her hair is pulled tightly back, and the corners of her lips pull downward. The portrait is typical of female poses at the time except for one small but essential detail: the threatening miniature hatchet pinned prominently on Nation's chest. This historic photograph serves as a memento not only of Carrie's visit but also of the fear and excitement she created in Crawfordsville for weeks during the summer of 1901.

Elizabeth Boynton Harbert and the Pursuit of Suffrage

Rebecca McDole

In the early nineteenth century, American women began to flock to a cause—suffrage. Equal rights became a rallying cry that spread slowly but surely until the Nineteenth Amendment gave women the vote in 1920. But without Crawfordsville's Elizabeth Boynton Harbert, suffrage may never have happened at all.

Elizabeth Morrison Boynton, born on April 15, 1843, was the oldest daughter of William and Abby (Sweetser) Boynton. William, from New Hampshire, and Abby, born in Boston, met in Indiana and were married in Indianapolis on April 30, 1841, by Reverend Henry Ward Beecher, minister of Second Presbyterian Church. Abby's uncle, Phillips Sweetser, was an Indianapolis lawyer who was associated with Beecher; Abby most likely accompanied Beecher to Indiana when he was bringing his family back from New England. The Boyntons settled in Crawfordsville and opened a store, selling dry goods, hardware and groceries. Frank Mills described William—or as Mills called him, Billy—as a "principal merchant" and "in every way…one of the best men who ever lived." Boynton's store, according to Mills, was the unofficial "headquarters" for Wabash College students. The Boyntons had one more daughter, Mary E., known as Mellie, in 1849. William Boynton died in 1852. Abby was remarried in 1853 to a clerk from William's store, Alvin Ramey, and the two had a son, William B. Ramey.

Education was a driving force in Elizabeth Boynton's life. Her work as a suffragist often focused on the importance of education for women if they were to gain equal rights. Elizabeth's education began in Crawfordsville at Miss Starr's School for Young Ladies and Misses. Miss Starr's School was located in the old Canby mansion at Jefferson Square; the building would be used as Central School until 1910, when it was replaced by the old Crawfordsville High School (which itself was extensively remodeled in 1993 to contain the Athena Center Senior Apartments, Athena Sport & Fitness and several other businesses). Elizabeth, or Lizzie as she was locally known, was listed in a handwritten general catalogue of students attending Miss Starr's school in the year 1846–47, along with Susan and Mary Elston, Mary Hovey and Anna Willson. An 1851 circular and catalogue of Miss Starr's School listed Lizzie in the Primary Department, the equivalent of today's elementary school, where her subjects were reading, spelling, arithmetic, geography, child's history and first lessons in natural philosophy. After Miss Starr married William White, son of Wabash president Charles White, and moved to New Orleans, Lizzie attended the Crawfordsville Female Seminary, where she added uranography (astronomy), physiology, ancient and modern history and rhetoric to her subjects. She went on to Western Female Seminary in Oxford, Ohio, in 1858 and eventually graduated with honors from Terre Haute Female College in 1862.

After graduation, Lizzie returned to Crawfordsville and began her career as an author. Her poem "Shadows Versus Sunbeams" appeared in *Wabash Magazine* in May 1864; Lizzie wrote about soldiers dying for their country and "toiling 'neath a Southern sun" and offered encouragement to prisoners of war. This subject was close to her heart—Lizzie's beau, William Soesbe Harbert, whom she met in 1860 at a social gathering hosted by Professor John L. Campbell of Wabash College, was a prisoner at Libby Prison in Richmond, Virginia. By 1867, Lizzie had published her first book, *The Golden Fleece*, and more importantly, she had found her life's passion: women's rights. Her article "Encouragement," from *Wabash Magazine* in June 1867, contained the seeds that would grow into Lizzie's life's work. "The writer of this article does not remember ever to have received a word of encouragement or advice in regard to her education from an unmarried man," Lizzie wrote, going on to point out that women had been successfully walking the line between a "domestic and a blue-stocking" and even going so far as to deal a staggering blow to that "foul thing," slavery, as Harriet Beecher Stowe did with *Uncle Tom's Cabin*. Lizzie urged the boys of Wabash to encourage and support the education of their sisters and wives, to help them on their "journey toward this new Mecca of woman's world."

Elizabeth Boynton Harbert in her thirties, after she had married William Soesbe Harbert and left Crawfordsville. The Harberts lived in Des Moines, Iowa, until 1874, when they moved to Evanston, Illinois, where William practiced law. In 1907, the family moved to Pasadena, California. *Boynton-Harbert Society*.

The next year, 1868, was a defining moment in Lizzie Boynton's life. On September 7, twenty-three women applied for admission to Wabash College, a traditionally all-male college. Lizzie and three friends, Mary Hannah Krout, Emma Hough Fairchild and Mary Cumberland Jennison, had previously been granted permission to attend Professor Campbell's physics lectures. Lizzie recalled in an interview with a Pasadena, California newspaper in 1915 that she had been promised by Wabash president Charles White that she could earn a diploma from the college. "This was in the morning…and that very night [October 29, 1861] he died suddenly from a stroke of apoplexy."

When the girls asked for diplomas again, they were not only denied, they were also offered the entirely unwelcome sympathy of the president and faculty. Mary Hannah Krout fired off an angry letter to the *Crawfordsville Weekly Journal* on October 8, 1868, in which she predicted that "the time will come, must come when the doors of Wabash shall open and we will enter." The girls were mocked in the *Weekly Journal* on October 22 when a tongue-in-cheek article agreed that they should be admitted, as long as the college would "fit up an exclusive kitchen presided over by a competent *professore de cuisine* in order that the young ladies may be educated for the positions that Heaven designed for them, competent wives and mothers." The first money Lizzie earned as an author, ten dollars, was paid her by the *New York Independent* for her account of the Wabash incident.

Lizzie was not deterred from her mission, though. In December, Lizzie and a group of like-minded ladies formed the Ladies' Reading Association (LRA), whose purpose was to offer a reading room and library for the exclusive use of women. To raise money for their library, the ladies gave a musical and literary entertainment on December 17 and 18, 1868. Lizzie appeared in a tableau, "The Spanish Gypsy," and earned good reviews from the *Weekly Journal*. In another tableau, "The Coming Woman," the ladies burlesqued themselves and their failed application to Wabash. The LRA was located in Mr. Wiley Kenyon's gallery located opposite the courthouse on Main Street and was outfitted with some of Mr. Kenyon's best pictures along with the *Atlantic*, *New Yorker* and the *Independent*. Lizzie was elected secretary that year; in 1869, she was elected president. The ladies gathered for discussions, readings, entertainments and book clubs. The purpose was not women's rights but rather an opportunity for women to educate themselves.

Under the auspices of the LRA, Lizzie wrote and delivered a lecture that would gain her national attention. The lecture, "Before Suffrage—What?" was delivered at McClelland Hall on January 28, 1869, and was so popular that she was asked to give it in Lafayette, then Cleveland and Cincinnati later that year. Mary A. Livermore described the Cincinnati presentation: "The speech of the day and evening was made by Lizzie Boynton, although among the speakers were Susan B. Anthony, Mrs. Stanton, and myself. She held the audience on the platform, as well as that in the hall, spellbound for over an hour," according to the *Encyclopedia of Illinois and History of Evanston*. But the subject of her lecture didn't always go over so well. While Lizzie was delivering her lecture in Crawfordsville in January, a box was left at the door with an old shirt, a hat and a pair of pants, with a sarcastic note attached. Lizzie's friend and fellow suffragist Anna Dickinson suggested that they return the favor with a bib and baby's dress.

Societies were forming across the country for the advancement of women, and Crawfordsville was called by the *Chicago Post* on May 6, 1869, the "headquarters for the Woman Suffrage movement in Hoosierdom." Lizzie Boynton was at the head of the movement. She attended the Equal Rights Convention in New York in May 1869; she helped organize the Woman's Suffrage Association in Crawfordsville in June, where she was elected president. A Woman's Rights Association of Indianapolis elected Lizzie vice-president. She and Dr. Mary Wilhite, one of the first women to practice medicine in Indiana, traveled to Chicago for the Woman Suffrage Convention on September 9, 1869, and on September 21, Lizzie was made the chairman of the Woman Suffrage Convention in Crawfordsville.

This picture of Elizabeth Boynton Harbert was taken in 1881, when she was thirty-eight years old. *Boynton-Harbert Society.*

The Crawfordsville convention began with an act of vandalism. The ladies decorated the Christian Church on the corner of Wabash Avenue and Walnut Street with evergreens, but the night before the meeting, the decorations were stolen; they were later found adorning the scaffolds of bricklayers on Elston corner. More controversy came later when Lizzie's friend and mentor, General Lew Wallace, was invited to speak. As he rose to speak, Mrs. Livermore asked permission from the chairman to speak after him; Wallace replied that he "supposed a woman always must have the last word." Wallace, in his remarks, ignored the purpose of the convention—suffrage—and spoke at great length in a condescending manner about Indiana divorce law. At one point, he suggested that there were never two women of the same opinion, to which Lizzie interrupted to say that Miss Susan B. Anthony and Mrs. Livermore were exceptions to that rule. Wallace "in a mimicking voice sneered at her," reported the *Crawfordsville Weekly Journal* on October 14, 1869. The ladies felt the general's speech was uncalled for and his sneer "beneath the dignity of a gentleman." Rumors abounded in the month to follow that Lizzie would run for Congress against Lew Wallace; the gossip had finally died down by January 1870.

Taken in 1895, this photo shows Elizabeth Boynton Harbert (far right), William Soesbe Harbert (second from right) and their children, Bess (third from left) and Corinne (with umbrella, center), near a mill on the road to Interlaken, Switzerland. In her later years, Elizabeth was an adherent to the spiritualist movement, or New Thought. Like the spiritualist heroine of her novel *Amore*, Elizabeth usually dressed in all white from the 1890s on, making this photo of a darkly clad Elizabeth unique. *Boynton-Harbert Society.*

Lizzie's writing didn't slow down amidst the conventions and meetings. She took over as editor of the "Coming Woman" column in the *Weekly Journal* in February 1870 and was preparing a Sunday school book the same month called "Only a Girl." Lizzie was still busy giving lectures, also, but her activities in Crawfordsville were winding down. On October 18, 1870, Lizzie married Civil War veteran and Wabash College graduate William Soesbe Harbert and moved with him to Des Moines, Iowa. Son Arthur Boynton Harbert was born in Des Moines on September 14, 1871, and daughter Corinne Boynton Harbert was born on September 30, 1873. The family moved to Evanston, Illinois, where daughter Boynton Elizabeth (Bess) Harbert was born on October 24, 1875.

Lizzie stayed active in the suffrage movement throughout her life, proving that a woman didn't have to choose between "domestic or blue-stocking." She was editor of the "Woman's Kingdom" column in the *Chicago Inter Ocean* for eight years and president of the Illinois Equal Suffrage Association for

Front row, left to right: Corinne Harbert and Elizabeth Boynton Harbert. *Back row, left to right*: Mary Harbert Rickards, Bess Harbert and William Soesbe Harbert. *Boynton-Harbert Society.*

twelve years. On June 11, 1884, Cincinnati Wesleyan College for Young Women conferred on her the degree of doctor of philosophy. Mrs. Elizabeth Boynton Harbert died in Pasadena, California, on January 19, 1925.

On October 2, 1869, the *Crawfordsville Weekly Review* reported that "there are probably no larger feet in the world than those to which the strong minded women of this country are attached." An enterprising reporter in Cincinnati ascertained shoe sizes of leading suffragists: "Mrs. Phelps wears fourteens, Miss Susan B. Anthony elevens, Mrs. Elizabeth Cady Stanton eights." Whatever her shoe size may have been, Elizabeth Boynton Harbert left big footprints in Montgomery County.

Ruth Morgan and the Waveland Vigilantes Foil a Robbery

Emily Griffin Winfrey

For two hours in the early morning of February 6, 1932, a small group of bank robbers worked to blow open the vault of the Waveland State Bank. Armed with high explosives and blasting nine shots of it within the bank, the criminals had not counted on Waveland's vigilante citizens. Within minutes of the first explosion, the bank was surrounded by the town's quick-reacting and heavily armed vigilantes. In the end, the combination of vigilante fire outside and the robbers' explosions inside nearly destroyed the bank's exterior and interior. But the robbers were both outsmarted and outnumbered. Because the citizens of Waveland courageously protected their bank, the robbers were unable to blow up the interior vault that held the money and ran away without a cent.

In the days after the robbery attempt, it was estimated that the total damage to the bank was $7,500. The damage was so bad that a large piece of the safe had been blown across the street and rested in the kitchen of the McIntire restaurant. The piece of steel landed in a sugar bowl, and despite the much larger damage across the street, the *Waveland Independent* lamented the bowl's "total loss" on February 12, 1932. The *Independent* and the *Crawfordsville Journal Review* covered the story with pride, and many Waveland residents were heralded as county heroes. The bank's assistant cashier, Theron Banta, and local businessmen Frank Gardner and George Slavens, each having taken close-range shots at the bank, were credited as

Waveland citizens survey the damage to the bank's exterior on February 6, 1932. A few hours before this photo was taken, a small group of robbers attempted to blow up the interior safe but were prevented by the town's vigilantes. The robbers' explosives and the vigilantes' bullets caused considerable damage. *North Salem State Bank.*

being the most successful of the vigilantes. The men took cover behind cars at Ben Canine's downtown garage and fired shots through the bank's front plate glass windows. The criminals inside the bank were also armed with shotguns, and their return fire narrowly missed the crouching businessmen. In addition to Banta, Gardner and Slavens, the *Journal Review* stated that about twenty local men, keeping a watchful eye on the bandits and steady fingers on their triggers, helped to prevent the robbery and any local injuries. Without the presence of vigilantes, the bank certainly would have been completely destroyed, as policemen from surrounding towns did not reach the scene until the shootout was over.

Although the vigilantes saved the bank, it was the quick response of those working at the telephone office, located two and a half blocks away, that led the vigilantes out of their homes and into the streets. Howard Worl, the telephone office manager, was awakened by the barking of his bulldog, Queen. Worl knew that something was amiss. At the same time, Ruth Morgan, twenty-two years old and nighttime telephone operator, realized that telephone lines were being cut because lights were going out inside the office. The February 6, 1932 *Journal Review* reported that the bandits cut telephone wires, broke streetlight bulbs and cut the rope to a nearby bell before entering the bank. As Ruth Morgan called townspeople to alert them of the situation, Howard Worl climbed a telephone

A *Journal Review* reporter (left) stands with vigilantes George Slavens (center) and Theron Banta (right) in front of the bank hours after the robbery attempt took place. Slavens and Banta had positioned themselves in proximity to the bank, and their shots scared the bandits away. These men were lauded as heroes. *North Salem State Bank.*

pole with a headset, planning to spread the word as he fixed the line. Atop the pole, Worl overheard the robbers discussing their getaway as they threw rocks at Queen, who was growling at the culprits. Dressed in white gloves and white pants, the bandits (eyewitnesses believed they saw seven men total) managed to flee in a getaway car that had been parked at J.V. Milligan's farm. The men (believed to be the same gang that had recently robbed the Roachdale Bank and the State Bank at Lizton) were never apprehended.

In the weeks following the attack, the February 26, 1932 *Independent* reported that the number of vigilantes increased, and many were sworn in as deputies to prevent any future robbery attempts. On April 15, it was announced that the Waveland Bank would operate out of the Alex Moore storeroom while steel lining, doors and an interior vault were replaced. By the end of May, the bank was back in its original building and was completely repaired, according to the May 20, 1932 *Independent.* Although the bank was restored, some of the proclaimed heroes lost their jobs later that summer. On August 5, the *Independent* announced that the Union Telephone Company decided to cut costs by asking Howard Worl to accept a 50 percent pay cut. Worl declined the pay cut in favor of retirement, and a new couple took charge of the exchange. Because the couple had two daughters and a son to run the exchange, Ruth Morgan and all the local girls employed at the telephone office lost their jobs.

The story of the Waveland Bank robbery became a thrilling tale of good guys outwitting the bad guys and appeared in national newspapers. With the

Residents view the interior damage of the Waveland bank. It would take three months to completely repair the bank and reopen for business. *North Salem State Bank.*

headline "Phone Girl Rouses Town to Save Bank," the *New York Times* singled out Ruth Morgan as the lone hero of the event. The February 7, 1932 *Times* reported that all the telephone lines leading outside of Waveland were cut by the robbers at about 2:20 a.m. Morgan "sensing the danger to her town and finding the local lines still working, called T.S. Banta…on his order, she summoned the protectors of the village to mobilize with their rifles." But the local newspaper chose a more surprising candidate as the most important figure of the event: Queen. If Ruth Morgan saved the bank by alerting the vigilantes, then Queen saved Morgan by alerting *her*! After naming individuals and praising their contributions, the *Journal Review* concluded on February 6 that "[i]t is believed locally that had not the dog commenced barking in the telephone office that the men would have taken the night operative captive and left this town of five hundred residents virtually without a means of communication with the outside world."

But after another harrowing event in 1939 and a television appearance in 1956, Ruth Morgan would always be associated with the courage she displayed as a young woman. Seven years after she bravely alerted townspeople of the Waveland Bank robbery, Morgan was kidnapped as she toured the Indiana State Prison in Michigan City. Ruth Morgan Joiner, then twenty-nine years old, had been working as a welfare worker in Crawfordsville for five months before she drew the largest stick to win a tour of the prison. Also along for the educational tour were Montgomery County Welfare Department director Nina Jones, state parole agent William Purdue and Tippecanoe County Welfare Department director Julia Snyder. As she toured the prison, a man grabbed Joiner's arm and said, "Right this way, lady." In the *Journal Review* on June 29, 1939, Joiner described the ordeal:

> *I didn't realize anything was wrong. I thought it was part of the tour. I walked into the office and was bewildered when they started to close the door…They sat me in a chair and threatened me as if I weren't human. I was frightened, but didn't scream. Then, they called the warden and made me talk to him. They kept threatening me. One would pull my head back by the hair and run the knife lightly across my throat. "That's what we'll do if you don't get guns for us," one said. I talked to the warden and told him that they would kill me unless he gave them guns, a car, and freedom. I pleaded with them and told them I had a little girl who needed me…it was a terrible, horrible experience.*

Ruth Morgan Joiner in a 1939 newspaper photo. Joiner, a telephone operator and later welfare worker, was noted for her courage during the Waveland Bank robbery and an Indiana State Prison capture. In the 1950s, she was honored on national television. *CDPL Photo.*

Ruth Joiner was held in captivity from about 10:30 a.m. until 1:00 p.m. After being threatened with butcher knives by the three prisoners for hours, it was the gunfire from her rescuers that injured her. The warden conversed with and distracted the convicts so that the state police were able to break into the office and shoot at the men. Although the state police officers' efforts captured the felons and freed Joiner, a stray bullet from the attack struck Joiner in the arm and chest.

After the 1930s ended, Ruth Morgan Joiner would move past the headline-grabbing attacks and instead be known as a much-loved teacher at the local Mount Zion school. But in 1956, the entire nation would learn of Joiner's heroic participation in both the Waveland Bank robbery and the Indiana State Prison capture. Kathryn Smith Bazzani believed that her cousin, Ruth Joiner, deserved to be highlighted on *This Is Your Life,* the popular television show hosted by Ralph Edwards that surprised guests by presenting their life story with participation from their friends and family. Bazzani wrote a letter nominating Joiner as a future participant on the show to Ralph Edwards and quickly received a form letter in return. Believing that her idea had been turned down, Bazzani was shocked when she received a telephone call from Edwards's office informing her that Joiner had been chosen for an upcoming show. Joiner thought she had been chosen to attend a teachers' training class at UCLA and sat in the *This Is Your Life* audience with Montgomery County's school superintendent John W. Ward and his wife, according to the *Tri-County News* of April 12, 1956. After reading her own name as the guest on Edwards's card, a very surprised and soft-spoken Joiner walked down to the stage, where her life was retold by the show's host and friends and family. Theron Banta, the celebrated vigilante of Waveland, made a special appearance and praised Mrs. Joiner for her brave actions during the bank robbery.

Karen Bazzani Zach, Kathryn's daughter, remembered watching the program as a child on top of someone's shoulders. The people of Waveland were excited to see one of their own, a woman Zach remembered as "one amazing lady, so sweet and kind," on television. Zach recalled that people gathered at the Bazzani house to watch together: "We had a whole house full of mostly relatives and a couple of couples from Waveland. We had a very large living room and it was full—at least twenty people if not more. I distinctly remember everyone yelling when Ruth was chosen out of the audience and when she walked across the stage and when her daughter, Jerry Lou, was on." Once she returned from California, Joiner was honored at a supper at Milligan Memorial Presbyterian Church in Crawfordsville. Joiner thanked the one hundred guests and showed them a book that included the entire script of the show, according to the May 3, 1956 *Tri-County News*. After being featured on television, Ruth Morgan Joiner, named the "best teacher in the whole world" by student Judith Dye on the NBC show, returned to teaching. According to her obituary in the June 1, 1987 *Journal Review*, Ruth Joiner Thomas taught at Waveland, Whitesville, East Union, Granville Wells, Mount Zion and Fountain Central Schools before retiring.

Ruth Morgan became a symbol of courage in the extraordinary experiences she encountered in her fairly ordinary positions at the telephone exchange and welfare office. Because of the many Waveland citizens who displayed courage during the attempted robbery, the bank still stands today. In the early morning hours of February 6, 1932, Waveland was full of Ruth Morgans—ordinary, dedicated people who risked their own lives to protect the future of their hometown.

Wabash College's Football Fatality

Rebecca McDole

Despite the dreary weather on October 21, 1910, the Wabash football team Little Giants were in good spirits as they left for St. Louis on the Vandalia line via Danville, Illinois. They had every reason to be optimistic—the season was shaping up to be a great one. They had already beaten Georgetown by 57 points and Purdue by 3, and just the week before, they had blown Butler away 48–0. Although guarding against what *The Bachelor* called the "Chicago Cubs malady" of overconfidence, the team and coaches expected to win, even though they had lost to St. Louis the previous year.

Much of the confidence felt by the Little Giants was inspired by the brilliant athletic ability of a few key players. Quarterback Kent "Skeet" Lambert, brother of legendary Purdue basketball coach Ward "Piggy" Lambert, played professional baseball after college before serving in World War I. "Indian Ed" Miller played halfback and later went on to success as a basketball coach and beloved teacher at Darlington. But the real star of the show was Round Hill native and 1909 Crawfordsville High School graduate Ralph Lee "Sap" Wilson.

Wilson played basketball and football for the Athenians; he was part of state championship–winning teams in both 1908 and 1909. He was chosen twice for all-state in both basketball and football. On October 24, 1910, the *Crawfordsville Daily Journal* called him "big and strong, and with unlimited nerve he attracted the attention of foot ball men all over the state

Ralph Lee Wilson's yearbook photograph from the 1910 *Athenian*. Ralph was president of his class from 1908 to 1909 and athletic editor of the yearbook. He also played football and basketball, ran track and was chosen by his class to give the commencement oration. *CDPL Photo.*

and several schools made strong efforts to secure him." Ralph Wilson was one of the best high school athletes in the state, and he chose the scarlet. In just the short time since school began in 1910, he proved himself on the field and off. He earned a starting spot on an undefeated football team, pledged Delta Tau Delta and was excelling at his studies. The *Daily Journal* called him "one of the most popular students in the college." After three or four bad seasons, things were looking up for football fans in Crawfordsville.

Football itself was looking quite different to fans since the first contest between Princeton and Rutgers in 1869. The sport was slowly morphing from rugby to a more unique and rugged contest that began to take shape when Walter Camp revised the rules in 1880. A scrimmage style of play was established, players were limited to eleven per side and, in 1882, Camp introduced a system of downs for advancing the ball. Public outcry in the late 1890s against the injuries and deaths common in football led to rules changes. This helped for a while, but the death rate began to climb again, and major reforms were necessary in the early 1900s. Seven players now lined up on the line of scrimmage across a neutral zone, a fourth official was added to keep an eye on the action and the game was reduced from seventy minutes to sixty (four fifteen-minute quarters). A first down now required ten yards instead of five, and the most innovative rule change in football history was invented: the forward pass. The rules committee, later the National Collegiate Athletic Association (NCAA), was focused on the safety of players. The year 1910 was the first full season to play under the new rules.

The day of the match between Wabash and St. Louis, October 22, was ideal except for the wind. As the players took the field, it was clear that Wabash

The 1909 Crawfordsville High School football team. Ralph Wilson is in the back row (far left). Ralph's high school teammate, Charles Merle Harlan (bottom row, second from left), played football with Ralph at Wabash. Another teammate, H. Grady Chadwick (top row, fourth from left), married Ralph's sister, Stella, in 1912. Grady Chadwick's brother, J. Frank Chadwick, was married to Ralph's other sister, Ethel, in 1900. *CDPL Photo.*

would have a size advantage: they outweighed the blue and white at least ten pounds to the man. Despite telling his roommate, Ross McCabe, that he had a bad feeling that someone was going to get hurt, Wilson's nervousness melted away as the game began. Four minutes into the first quarter, "Sap" ran thirty yards for a touchdown. Although fumbles and penalties were abundant on both sides, St. Louis found the Wabash boys unstoppable. The *Daily Journal* reported on October 24 that "Coach Harper's boys had a way of tackling that not only proved certain but also made the varsity players realize the fact that they were up against the best trained bunch of foot ball men they had ever met." While St. Louis made use of the forward pass frequently (eight attempts, one successful), Wabash only made two tries and failed both times. A poor pass by St. Louis in the last quarter gave Frederick "Fritz" Eglin a chance to score, and Wabash won, 10–0.

At least three players were injured in the game: St. Louis' Painter hurt his leg catching an attempted on-side kick, "Indian Ed" Miller of Wabash hurt his shoulder and Ralph Wilson received a blow to the head but appeared to be fine. "Skeet" Lambert called a trick play in the third quarter, a fake end run in which a wedge was sent around an end to mislead the other team and a halfback (Ralph) slipped through an opening made by a guard. A St. Louis player, recognizing the subterfuge, stepped into the opening, and Wilson, "hurtling forward at a tremendous speed, crashed against his knee, fracturing his skull," according to the *Crawfordsville Daily Journal* of October 25, 1910. Wilson was knocked out, but the *Daily Journal* reported that he immediately regained consciousness, staggering to his feet and asking team captain "Sis" Hopkins for a timeout. Despite reports by the *St. Louis Globe Democrat* that Coach Harper left Ralph unattended and ignored on the sidelines, he was actually helped to the gymnasium changing room by teammate Don Irvin and took a taxi back to the American Hotel. *The Bachelor* reported on October 29 that Wilson was unconscious when he arrived back at the hotel but woke up asking, "Did Wabash win?"

The rest of the Wabash team, assured that "Sap" would be fine, headed home after the game, leaving team manager Harry Eller to bring Ralph back to Crawfordsville later. At about eleven o'clock that night, Ralph lost consciousness again and was taken to Josephine Hospital, where it was discovered that he had blood clots on his brain, necessitating surgery. Harry Eller telegraphed Ralph's father that his condition was serious. James D. Wilson, Coal Creek Township trustee and former county commissioner, was reportedly "always fearful that he [Ralph] would be injured in football and begged him to quit the game." But the *Daily Journal* also reported on October 24 that he "was proud of his boy's athletic achievements" and attended every home game in which his son played. Wilson was concerned when Ralph didn't return with the rest of the boys, and upon receiving word from Eller, he immediately went to St. Louis on the Big Four and Wabash line. Ralph's father arrived at 8:15 p.m. but was too late. Ralph had died of his head injury two hours earlier.

Ralph Wilson's death was devastating to his family, friends and teammates and had a profound effect on the entire town of Crawfordsville. By unspoken consent, the rest of the football season was cancelled. The high school athletic association met and voted to cancel Crawfordsville High School's football season; with no knowledge of this, the high school players met and resolved to play no more. Five Butler players—Joe and Dan Mullane, Chester Marsh, Joe Peak and Xerxes Silver—quit football out of grief for Ralph. Wabash professors Thomas, Osborne, Garner and Daniels called on Ralph's mother at Round Hill to express the sympathy of the whole college. Kent Lambert, quarterback of the Wabash team, never got over his grief and guilt over calling the play that killed his friend, according to his daughter, Jeanne Ann Vanderhoef. Decades later, he still shed tears at the memory, while his wife, Janet Lambert (the former Maude Snyder and Ralph Wilson's fiancée at the time of his death), found it too painful to speak of Ralph at all.

Ralph's headstone at Oak Hill Cemetery bears his last words, "Did Wabash Win?" In a letter of gratitude for the sympathy of the town after Ralph's death, James D. Wilson wrote in the *Daily Journal* on November 5, 1910: "We feel grateful to all, we blame no one, we bow to the inevitable, and…think of him as 'only gone on ahead—just around the bend.'" *CDPL Photo.*

James Wilson and Harry Eller brought Ralph's body home on October 24. They were met at Terre Haute by Wabash president Dr. G.L. Mackintosh, Professor D.D. Hains, Ralph's two uncles and his fraternity brothers, John McClamroch, Ward Lambert and T.H. Ristine. Waiting at the train station in Crawfordsville was the entire Wabash student body, faculty, Crawfordsville High School students and family friends. "With heads uncovered the student body then escorted the remains of their friend and brother student" home to Round Hill. Two funerals were held; the first was at the family's home, with Ralph's six cousins acting as pallbearers. Five hundred people attended the first service, and even more turned out for the service that afternoon at First Methodist Episcopal Church in Crawfordsville. At this second service, members of Ralph's football team—J.F. Cravens, M.E. Elliott, F.E. Ebert, O.L. Barr, Ray Hopkins, S.T. Starbuck, Merle Harlan, Kent Lambert, Leroy Gangwisch and Ed Miller—were pallbearers. College students and high school boys marched two abreast from the church to Oak Hill Cemetery, where Ralph was buried.

Plans for a memorial to Ralph Wilson began immediately. By December 10, though, the memorial committee had done nothing, blaming the grieving chairman Kent Lambert's repeated failure to call a meeting. On January 18, 1911, *The Bachelor* reported that the committee, now in Chairman Harris's charge, had selected Indianapolis sculptor Rudolf Schwarz to design the memorial. Schwarz also designed the Veterans' Memorial at the Montgomery County Courthouse and part of the Soldiers' and Sailors' Monument in Indianapolis. Collections for the memorial began on February 4. Finally, in a ceremony at Wabash College on April 22, 1911, a bronze tablet bearing

The memorial to Ralph Lee Wilson is now located in the central entrance of the Little Giant Stadium. According to a *Bachelor* article from 1975, the memorial was originally placed in Yandes Library and was later rescued from obscurity in the gymnasium by Athletic Director Max Servies. It is not known how or when the plaque was moved to the gymnasium; it has been in its present spot at the stadium since the early 1970s. *CDPL Photo.*

Ralph's name, birth and death dates and the words "Pro Collegio" was placed in the east reading room of the college library. It was later moved and now resides in Hollett Stadium.

As much as football has changed since Ralph Wilson's death, concussions and fatal head injuries are still major concerns at all levels of the game. Leather helmets have given way to hard plastic, thick padding and face masks. Wilson played at an especially violent time; fourteen men died from football-related injuries in 1910. Even the intrepid President Theodore Roosevelt, hunter of lions and hero of the Spanish-American War, found the sport too fierce for his taste and called for reforms in 1905. While football continues to evolve to protect players, the memory of Ralph "Sap" Wilson, warrior of the gridiron, lives on at Wabash College.

MARY ODA EGLIN, "ARTIST OF THE ARMY AIR CORPS"

Jodie Steelman Wilson

In 1903, when Crawfordsville artist Mary Oda was given honorary membership in the Art League of Montgomery County at the age of sixteen, it is unlikely that local residents were surprised by her talent. Both her mother and grandfather had earned their livings as artists in Crawfordsville. But unlike her family members, she would go on to a career outside Montgomery County and eventually gain fame as the "Artist of the Army Air Corps" for her work painting portraits of the pilots of the U.S. Army Air Corps, the forerunner to today's U.S. Air Force.

Born on October 8, 1886, in Crawfordsville, Mary's parents divorced just six months after her birth. Her mother, Jennie Oda, raised her children in the household of Jennie's parents, Harriet (Ramey) Dixon and Jacob Dixon. Harriet's stepsister was Elizabeth Boynton Harbert, the Crawfordsville suffragette.

Being raised in a household with two artists surely influenced Mary's childhood, and her obituary claimed that she began to paint when she was only eight years old. During this time, her mother was earning a living as a crayon artist, according to the 1895 Crawfordsville city directory. Before her eleventh birthday, Mary was displaying her own crayon sketches in a display at Lacey's Store, dealers in books and art supplies, located at 123 East Main Street. The August 28, 1897 edition of the *Crawfordsville Daily Argus News* remarked on the display and noted that Mary Oda "possesses considerable artistic ability."

Photograph of Mary Oda, art instructor at Crawfordsville High School, taken from the 1914 *Athenian* yearbook, which was dedicated to the young teacher. The first page of the yearbook bore the inscription, "With sincerest appreciation of her loyalty and of her unselfish labor for C.H.S., this tenth volume of the *Athenian* is lovingly dedicated by the class of 1914 to Miss Mary Oda." *CDPL Photo.*

She graduated from Crawfordsville High School in 1905, and her first-known surviving work dates from this time, painted for a friend in 1906. The painting, *Ben-Hur Beeches*, was given by Mary Oda as a graduation gift and was later donated to the Montgomery County Historical Society, where it is on display at the time of this writing.

Mary studied at the Chicago Art Institute—where fellow Crawfordsville artist, Theodora Larsh, was a classmate in the Department of Painting and Drawing—and then attended Chicago University in 1912. When she returned to Crawfordsville, she became an art teacher at the high school, where she proved so popular that, upon resigning, the June 11, 1915 *Crawfordsville Daily Journal* reported that "the announcement of Miss Oda's resignation was quite unlooked for by the school authorities and was accepted only because she persisted so much…great sympathy is extended to the class of 1916, which will be without her assistance."

Sometime after 1911, Mary met Wabash College student Frederick Eglin, who routinely studied at her family's kitchen table. Family stories tell of Frederick's early history: his parents were Swiss immigrants to New York City and died when Frederick was young. Without his parents to provide for him, he may even have been homeless for a time. One day, an alumnus of Wabash College noticed him playing a pickup ballgame in a park and made it possible for him to attend Wabash, where he became a star athlete on the football, basketball and baseball teams. Shortly after he had enrolled at Wabash, his benefactor died, so he worked his way through school by waiting tables in fraternity houses at Wabash, firing furnaces and doing other odd jobs in Crawfordsville.

In 1915, when Mary departed for New York to study at an art institute and pursue her painting career in the center of the art world, Frederick had already graduated from Wabash. After graduation, he was deployed to Texas with the Indiana National Guard to monitor the border with Mexico. In early 1917, after attaining the rank of sergeant major of the Second Indiana Infantry, he passed the examination for lieutenancy in the U.S. Aviation Corps, an elite group of pilots. Eglin, awaiting the test results in Crawfordsville, left almost immediately for New York to see Mary upon hearing the news. He was appointed second lieutenant in the Indiana National Guard, with a pay increase to $210 per month plus expenses during his aviation training.

Mary Oda, possibly during her years in New York. *Collection of the Frederick I. Eglin and Mary Oda Eglin family.*

Eglin was sent to aviation school in California and soon became a very good pilot, according to local reports published in the *Daily Journal*. The training wasn't without its risks, however, and the newspaper reported on November 9, 1917, that Eglin had been thrown through the windshield of his airplane and had received cuts on his face and hands. He was undeterred by the injuries and did not miss a moment of his training. This accident was not his first; on another occasion, he crash-landed his airplane. The accident had been observed at a distance, and an ambulance was immediately sent to pick him up. Eglin refused the ambulance, preferring to walk back to his quarters without assistance.

By the time he and Mary Oda were married in New York on August 13, 1918, he had attained the rank of captain. Although Mary left New York to accompany her husband to his future duty stations, she did not abandon her painting. Instead, she chose subjects close at hand as outlets for her artistic expression. Surrounded by the pioneer aviators in the U.S. Army Air Service, later renamed the U.S. Army Air Corps, Mary Oda Eglin was commissioned by many pilots to paint their portraits. Whether they were stationed in the Philippines, California, Texas or Virginia, Mary's artistic skills were in demand.

Mary Oda Eglin's obituary, which appeared in the *Crawfordsville Journal Review* on November 13, 1939, provided no source for this quote attributed to

Mary Oda Eglin, Frederick Jr. and Frederick Eglin Sr., holding Harriet Jane. This photo was taken in 1922 while the family was living in the Philippines. *Collection of the Frederick I. Eglin and Mary Oda Eglin family.*

her: "Every time I changed stations, I was forced to leave behind unfinished pictures. Always I worked frantically from the time my husband received orders for his next detail until the last moment before leaving the field, trying to finish, in the face of military orders, work that I must deliver before leaving."

A portrait of Horace Hickam, a native of Spencer, Indiana, is likely the most well known of Mary's works. Hickam, an air corps aviator who began his career in 1917, later wrote the first history of the air service, the predecessor to the air corps. He was killed in a flight accident in 1934. Mary Oda Eglin was commissioned to paint Hickam's portrait from a photograph for placement at the newly named Hickam Field, located next to Pearl Harbor in Hawaii, upon completion of her work. In 1941, the portrait of Hickam survived the Japanese bombing of Pearl Harbor and Hickam Field. The base suffered 139 deaths, 303 injuries and extensive damage to planes and property, a key objective to prevent rapid U.S. retaliation against the Japanese forces following the attack.

Another portrait, one of army officer Colonel Beaumont Buck, painted during the Eglins' time in San Antonio, was praised at a private showing of Mary Oda Eglin's works held at the Menger Hotel in 1927. This historic Texas hotel was known as the location where Teddy Roosevelt recruited his Rough Riders for service in Cuba in 1898. The portrait of Buck was ultimately hung in the state Senate chamber in Austin, Texas. While in San Antonio, Mary Oda Eglin studied under Jose Arpa, a Spanish painter known for his realistic style and skill in painting sunlight. Although she likely painted hundreds of portraits and landscapes during her career, no detailed biographical information or comprehensive list of her works has previously been made readily available to researchers.

While Mary was devoting time to improving her artistic skills, Frederick devoted his to aviation and developing his leadership skills. While attending the Command and General Staff School, Eglin wrote a paper about whether attack aviation should be considered a separate discipline from general aviation, and his ideas on tactics and strategy contributed much to the development of American military aviation. He seemed headed on a path of increasing recognition and responsibility in the military and was likely to receive further advancement in rank.

On New Year's Day 1937, on a routine flight, Frederick Eglin left Langley Field, Virginia, with U.S. Navy officer Lieutenant Howard Shelton en route to Maxwell Field, Alabama. The conditions were poor for a flight: heavy rains and fog obscured the top of the highest peak in Alabama, Cheaha Mountain. With visibility severely restricted, the plane crashed into pine

The official service portrait of Lieutenant Colonel Frederick I. Eglin, for whom the largest air force base in the United States is named. Despite his birth in New York City and adulthood spent in military assignments, he still considered Crawfordsville "home." *Collection of the Frederick I. Eglin and Mary Oda Eglin family.*

trees on the mountain peak and burst into flames, killing both Eglin and Shelton. An army investigating board found that the men had died in the line of duty. Eglin was interred at Arlington National Cemetery. In August 1937, the U.S. War Department renamed the flying field at Valparaiso, Florida, Eglin Field in his honor. Today, Eglin Air Force Base is the largest in the United States.

Mary was left to raise their two children, Frederick, Jr. and Harriet Jane. Within a few months of her husband's death, Mary's mother passed away in Evansville, Indiana. About this time, Mary became ill with what the family now believes was a cancer of the digestive tract. Friends who had watched her paint for years wondered if a habit she had of placing her paintbrush in her mouth to form a point was responsible for her condition. Artists' paints at the time frequently contained lead and other hazardous ingredients. Despite her illness, she lived in Washington, D.C., with her children as long as she was able to manage their care. Soon, however, it was evident that something further had to be done.

Her children were sent away to boarding schools; Harriet Jane was a student at Blackstone Academy in Virginia, and Frederick Jr. went to Camp Dix, New Jersey, to prepare for the United States Military Academy. Friends of the now struggling family were members of the Order of Daedalians, an organization of military pilots, as Frederick Eglin had been, and the order members took care of the children's tuition by creating scholarships to fund their study. The children also worked to pay fees not covered by the scholarships.

Harriet Jane Eglin, portrayed in the hills behind the Eglin home in California. Streaks from the water used to fight the fire that killed Mary Oda Eglin are visible in the original painting. *Collection of the Frederick I. Eglin and Mary Oda Eglin family.*

In a final tragedy, though, Mary Oda Eglin was killed in a fire, perhaps started by a cigarette, in her Washington, D.C., apartment on November 11, 1939. According to friends in Crawfordsville, her years in Washington were very busy ones, and she had been overworking herself. She was buried at her husband's side at Arlington National Cemetery. Many paintings that remained in her home were streaked by the water from firemen's hoses as they extinguished the fire. A number of paintings were either taken by, or given to, neighbors who had helped the family through Mary's illness.

A family friend, General Eugene Reinartz, accepted guardianship of the children and saw to their care. Harriet Jane finished art school and married a combat pilot. Like her mother, she had great artistic ability, painted both commissioned and freelance works and traveled the world with her military husband. She and her husband had seven children. Frederick Eglin Jr. graduated from West Point and piloted fifteen B-17 missions over Germany during World War II. He was shot down, captured and kept in a German prisoner of war camp. He spent several years in a hospital recovering from his wounds. He married the nurse who had cared for him during his hospital stay, and they had three sons. He received the Peace Medal, the highest peacetime valor award, for risking his life to save an aircraft and its crew.

The Eglin family has had a lasting effect on the development of what is now the U.S. Air Force, and Mary Oda Eglin's artistic ability has provided generations with portraits of the pioneers of aviation, many of whom were killed in the line of duty. The impact of this family remains through the military tactical contributions of Frederick Eglin Sr., the enduring beauty of the art of Mary Oda Eglin and the many descendants of this couple, some still serving their country in our armed forces. But although Eglin is now a household word across the country and across the world, it was Crawfordsville, Indiana, that the couple called their hometown.

Sources

Essential sources for this book include many newspapers and periodicals published in Montgomery County and elsewhere from the 1850s to the present. Within the chapters, these sources are cited. Due to space constraints, only major sources are included in the source list. Individuals who have provided supporting information have been listed in our acknowledgements. The authors conducted interviews with many individuals who are named within each chapter.

The following Crawfordsville publications were consulted in our research: *Star*, *Daily News Review*, *Daily Journal*, *Journal Review*, *Review*, *Daily Argus News*, *Weekly Argus*, *Weekly Review* and *Weekly Journal*. Other local sources included the *Waveland Independent* and the *Tri-County News*. Lafayette (Indiana) newspapers included the *Lafayette Weekly Argus* and the *Lafayette Daily Courier*. Many nonlocal publications were also consulted, including the *San Jose (CA) News*, *Los Angeles Times*, *New York Times*, *San Francisco Call*, *San Francisco Chronicle*, *San Jose (CA) Evening News* and *Spokane (WA) Spokesman-Review*.

Ancestry.com databases were also consulted in our research.

The Bachelor. Student Weekly of Wabash College, 1908.

Banta, Richard E. *Crawfordsville: One Hundred Forty-Three Years in the Hoosier Athens*. Crawfordsville, IN: Crawfordsville Area Centennial Corporation, 1965.

Bateman, Newton, Paul Selby, Harvey B. Hurd and Robert D. Sheppard, eds. *Historical Encyclopedia of Illinois and History of Evanston*. Vol. 2. Chicago: Munsell Publishing Company, 1906, 559–62.

Bausch and Lomb Optical Company. *The Bausch & Lomb Lens Souvenir.* Rochester, NY: self-published, 1903.

Beckwith, H.W. *History of Montgomery County.* Chicago: H.H. Hill and N. Iddings, 1881.

Bowen, A.W. *History of Montgomery County, Indiana.* Indianapolis, IN: A.W. Bowen, 1913.

Boynton, Lizzie M. "Encouragement." *Wabash Magazine* (June 1867).

———. "Shadows Versus Sunbeams." *Wabash Magazine* (May 1864).

Cantrell, Martha. *The Quilt Chronicles: A Montgomery County Heritage, 1821–1979.* Crawfordsville, IN: Montgomery County Historical Society and Crawfordsville Art League, 1979.

Cline, Pat. *Crawfordsville: A Pictorial History.* St. Louis, MO: G. Bradley Publishing, 1991.

Cline, Pat, ed. *Montgomery County Legend and Lore.* Crawfordsville, IN: Montgomery County Historical Society, 1988.

Counts, I. Wilmer, and Jon Dilts. *The Magnificent 92 Indiana Courthouses*. Bloomington, IN: Rosebud Press, 1991.

Crane, Cheryl. *Detour: A Hollywood Story*. New York: Avon, 1989.

De Regniers, Beatrice Schenk. "Beatrice Schenk de Regniers." *Something about the Author Autobiography Series.* Vol. 6. Detroit, MI: Gale, 1988, 103–119.

Eglin family papers (reproductions). Eglin Family Collection. Crawfordsville District Public Library, Crawfordsville, Indiana.

Elliott, John. The Maurine Dallas Watkins Website. http://www.maurinewatkins.com.

Encyclopedia Britannica. "History of Photography." http://www.britannica.com/EBchecked/topic/457919/photography-history-of.

Fink, Paul. "Alf Lookabill Has Art World of His Own, Fashioned by Himself, All Out of Gourds." *Indianapolis Sunday Star*, May 25, 1924.

Freedman family papers. Freedman/De Regniers Collection. Crawfordsville District Public Library Local History, no. 20110716.

Gronert, Theodore. *Sugar Creek Saga: A History and Development of Montgomery County*. Crawfordsville, IN: Wabash College, 1958.

Guiley, Rosemary Ellen. *The Encyclopedia of Ghosts and Spirits*. 3rd ed. New York: Checkmark Books, 2007.

Hartmann, Sadakichi. "The Salon Club and the First American Photographic Salon at New York." *American Amateur Photographer* 15, no.7 (July 1904): 296.

Harvey, Robert, ed. *These Fleeting Years: Wabash College 1832–1982*. Crawfordsville, IN: Wabash College, 1982.

Hawaii Aviation. "Hickam Field." http://hawaii.gov/hawaiiaviation/hawaii-airfields-airports/oahu-pre-world-war-ii/hickam-field-air-force-base.

Helling, William P. *Images of America: Crawfordsville, IN*. Charleston, SC: Arcadia Publishing, 2011.

Herr family papers (reproductions). Herr Family Collection. Crawfordsville District Public Library, Crawfordsville, Indiana.

Herr, John. *Shirl, My Brother*. Edited by Dale Edward Linvill. N.p., n.d.

Hoffman, F., ed. *The Revised Montgomery County Atlas*. Crawfordsville: Indiana Printing Company, 1898.

Kirtley, James Marion. *Kirtley Kronicles: The Life and Times of James Marion Kirtley, M.D.* Crawfordsville, IN: R.R. Donnelley and Sons, 1997.

Ladies' Home Journal 16, no. 1. "The Gossip of the Editors" (December 1898).

Lambert, Janet. "Former City Woman Remembers Town, Residents." *Crawfordsville Journal Review*, December 1, 1976.

Livingston, David. "Meticulous Care, Quiet Excitement: Preludes to Flight." *Lafayette Journal and Courier*, June 3, 1961.

Lookabill, H. Randel. Gourd Museum scrapbook and papers. Crawfordsville District Public Library, Crawfordsville, Indiana.

Looking for Mabel Normand. "Who Was Ferris Hartman?" http://looking-for-mabel.webs.com/ferrishartman.htm.

Mitchell, Guy E. "Notes from Washington, D.C." *Massachusetts Ploughman and New England Journal of Agriculture* (March 10, 1906).

Montgomery: Your County Magazine. Monthly supplement to *Crawfordsville Journal Review*, 1976–99.

Montgomery County. "Ruth Morgan." Indiana GenWeb Project: Montgomery County, http://ingenweb.org/inmontgomery/bios/m/morgan-ruth.htm.

Moser, James Henry. "The First American Photographic Salon." *Washington Post*, January 15, 1905.

Neideffer, Rebecca L. *Court House to Be Erected for Montgomery County in Crawfordsville, Indiana*. Crawfordsville: Indiana Printing Co., Inc. 1987.

New York Times. "Done with the Big Toe: Margaret Fox Kane Shows How Spirit Rapping Is Produced." October 22, 1888.

Nicholson, Kenyon. "Ben Hur." Letter to the Editor. *Life* 47 (December 7, 1959): 20.

Norberg, John. *Wings of Their Dreams: Purdue in Flight.* West Lafayette, IN: Purdue University, 2003.

Ogle, George A., ed. *Standard Atlas of Montgomery County, Indiana*. Chicago: Geo. A. Ogle and Company, 1917.

Pasadena Star-News. "Death Calls Pioneer of Suffrage." January 19, 1925.

Perry, Douglas. *The Girls of Murder City: Fame, Lust, and the Beautiful Killers Who Inspired Chicago*. New York: Viking, 2010.

Riggs, Connie K. "The Man and the Tower Clock." *Northwestern Jeweler*, December 1977.

Riggs, Connie K., ed. *Montgomery County Remembers*. Crawfordsville, IN: Montgomery County Historical Society and Crawfordsville Community Bicentennial Committee, 1976.

Rohrbough, Malcolm J. *The Land Office Business: The Settlement and Administration of American Public Lands, 1789–1837*. New York: Oxford University Press, 1968.

Rose, Irv. "Freedmans: Interview with Harry and Sophia Freedman." Transcript available from the Crawfordsville District Public Library Local History Image database, http://history.cdpl.lib.in.us/images/20110804-1002.pdf.

Ross, Malcolm. "Balloon Ride to the Edge of Space." *National Geographic* (November 1961).

Schallert, Edwin. "Idol of Youth Puts Baby Before Films." *Los Angeles Times*, November 7, 1943.

Schudel, Matt. "Lillian F. Goldman, Artist, 98." *Washington Post*, March 8, 2009.

Servies, Max. *Wabash College All-Time Athletic Records Since 1867*. Crawfordsville, IN: Max Servies, 1971.

Stockinger, Anna. "The History of Spiritualism in Indiana." *Indiana Magazine of History* 20 (March–December 1924): 280–87.

Stoll, John B. *History of the Indiana Democracy, 1816–1916*. Indianapolis: Indiana Democratic Publishing Company, 1917.

This Is Your Life. Episode no. YLN189, first broadcast April 11, 1956, by NBC. Directed by Axel Gruenberg.

Thomas, Shirley. "Malcolm D. Ross." *Men of Space: Profiles of the Leaders in Space Research, Development, and Exploration*. Vol. 4. Philadelphia, PA: Chilton Company, 1962, 136–69.

Turner, Lana. *Lana: The Lady, the Legend, the Truth*. New York: Dutton, 1982.

U.S. War Department. *General Orders, No. 6.* Washington, D.C., August 4, 1937.

Voices of an Era...2. Special supplement to the *Crawfordsville Journal Review*, November 30, 1999.

Wabash Magazine. "The Twenty-Three." December 1869.

Walters, Crystal Pauline Randel. *Fredericksburg (Mace) and Mace Station (Linnsburg) and Vicinity, Montgomery County, Indiana, 1823 to 1969.* Fort Wayne, IN: Fort Wayne Public Library, 1971.

Watkins, Maurine. *Chicago*. Edited by George Jean Nathan. New York: Alfred A. Knopf, 1927.

Watterson, John Sayle. *College Football: History, Spectacle, Controversy.* Baltimore, MD: Johns Hopkins University Press, 2000.

Wikipedia. "Malcolm Ross (balloonist)." http://en.wikipedia.org/wiki/Malcolm_Ross_(balloonist).

Williams, George Thomas. *Pioneer Physicians and Surgeons of Montgomery County, Indiana.* Indianapolis: Indiana State Medical Association, 1945. Reprinted from the *Journal of the Indiana State Medical Association* 36, no. 5 (May 1943): 268–69; 36, no. 9 (September 1943): 517–19; 36, no. 11 (November 1943): 608–611; 37, no. 7 (July 1944): 372–74; and 37, no. 12 (August 1944): 697–702.

Wise, John. *A System of Aeronautics.* Philadelphia, PA: J.A. Speel, 1850.

Wylie, Charles Clayton. "Did a Meteorite Strike the Crawfordsville Ford?" *Scientific American* 144 (March 1931): 232.

———. "Fireballs Reported to the University of Iowa." *Popular Astronomy* 39 (1931): 222.

———. "A Proposed Sky Patrol by the Meteoritical Society." *Popular Astronomy* 56 (1948): 217.

Zach, Karen Bazzani. *Crawfordsville: Athens of Indiana.* Charleston, SC: Arcadia Publishing, 2003.

Index

M

N

O

P

R

S

T

About the Authors

Jodie Steelman Wilson is a reference and local history librarian at the Crawfordsville District Public Library, Crawfordsville, Indiana. She received a bachelor's degree in journalism from the University of Illinois, Urbana-Champaign, and a master's degree in library science from Indiana University–Indianapolis. She enjoys applying journalistic approaches to historical subjects to illuminate local history and has written for many publications. She lives with her husband, Michael, and daughters, Annie and Alison, in rural Indiana.

Emily Griffin Winfrey is a reference and local history librarian at the Crawfordsville District Public Library in Crawfordsville, Indiana. She received a bachelor's degree in communication from Wingate University in Wingate, North Carolina, and a master's degree in library and information science from Drexel University in Philadelphia, Pennsylvania. She is a member of the Society of Indiana Archivists. She has written local history articles for *Montgomery County Memories* and *Wabash Magazine*. She lives with her husband, Russell, in Montgomery County.

Rebecca McDole is a reference and local history librarian at the Crawfordsville District Public Library, Crawfordsville, Indiana, and also a bookseller at Barnes & Noble, Lafayette, Indiana. She received her bachelor's at Purdue in English/creative writing with a minor in history. She received her master's in library science from Indiana University–Indianapolis. Rebecca is a member of the American Library Association. She has published several articles in *Montgomery County Memories* and has several more in the queue.